Exploring America's Great Loop

Exploring America's Great Loop

Artfully Cruising the Rivers and Canals of North America

James & Jill Iverson

SEAWORTHY PUBLICATIONS, INC. • MELBOURNE, FLORIDA

Exploring America's Great Loop
Artfully Cruising the Rivers and Canals of North America
Copyright ©2024 by James & Jill Iverson

Published in the USA by:
Seaworthy Publications, Inc.
6300 N Wickham Rd.
Unit #130-416
Melbourne, FL 32940
Phone 321-389-2506
e-mail orders@seaworthy.com
www.seaworthy.com

All rights reserved. No part of this book may be reproduced, stored in a retrieval system, or transmitted in any form, or by any means, electronic, mechanical, photocopying, recording, or by any storage and retrieval system, without permission in writing from the publisher.

Library of Congress Cataloging-in-Publication Data

Names: Iverson, James, 1950- author. | Iverson, Jill, 1957- author.
Title: Exploring America's Great Loop : artfully cruising the rivers and canals of North America / James & Jill Iverson.
Description: Melbourne, Florida : Seaworthy Publications, Inc., 2024. | Summary: "Join James and Jill on a year-long journey of discovery as they joyously experience the challenges and rewards of America's Great Loop. Illustrated with pages from Jill's sketch journal, it is a fun, enlightening read for anyone interested in the magic of traveling by water. It is also a great source of information about transiting the Great Loop in your own boat"-- Provided by publisher.
Identifiers: LCCN 2024011194 (print) | LCCN 2024011195 (ebook) | ISBN 9781948494946 (paperback) | ISBN 9781948494953 (kindle edition)
Subjects: LCSH: Boats and boating--Atlantic Coast (U.S.) | Boats and boating--Great Lakes Region (North America) | Boats and boating--Tennesee River. | Boats and boating--Mississippi River. | Iverson, James, 1950---Travel--United States. | Iverson, Jill, 1957---Travel--United States.
Classification: LCC GV776.A84 I84 2024 (print) | LCC GV776.A84 (ebook) | DDC 797.10975--dc23/eng/20240326
LC record available at https://lccn.loc.gov/2024011194
LC ebook record available at https://lccn.loc.gov/2024011195

Dedication

To friends we left at home, to friends we met along the way, and to friends that virtually shared our adventure.

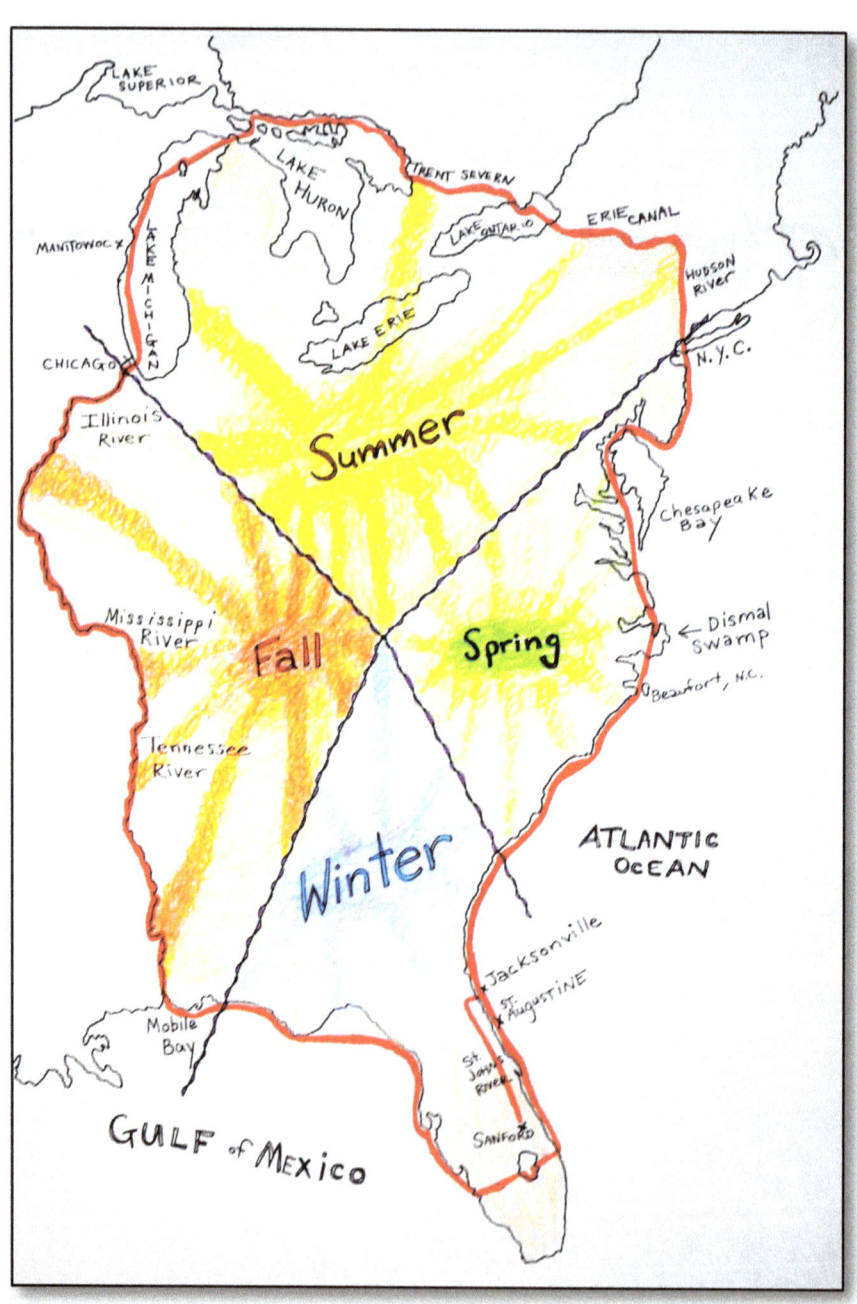

Contents

Dedication V

Introduction VIII

Prologue X

From the Great Lakes to the Gulf Coast 1

The Gulf Coast and Florida 29

Up the Atlantic Coast 56

To New York and the Canals 80

Georgian Bay and the North Channel 105

The Great Lakes and Home 114

Epilogue 119

Acknowledgments 121

About the Authors 122

Introduction

The Great Loop is a North American boating adventure. Using a combination of rivers, canals, lakes, and open ocean passages it is a circumnavigation of the eastern third of the United States and part of Canada. The nature of a loop means you finish where you start. There are no hard and fast rules; you begin your journey when and where you wish and take as much time or as little time as you want. The lack of rules does not mean there are no established conventions. Most loopers (the accepted term for people on the Great Loop) travel in a counterclockwise direction to take advantage of the currents on the great rivers of middle America. Planning your route with consideration of seasonal weather is the conventional wisdom. Travel south on the rivers to the gulf in the Fall. Spend the Winter traveling around Florida. Head North along the Atlantic coast in the Spring and enjoy Canada and the Great Lakes in the Summer. In theory this schedule might keep you in seventy-degree temperatures all year. Reality dictates there will be some hot sweltering days and other days when jackets and sweaters are required.

Our loop took a year, and we did it in one continuous voyage. Some people do it much faster. Some break it up into easily digestible sections and let the adventure unfold over many years. Our leisurely pace made generous allowances for lingering a week or so at some locations that we both found intriguing.

Transiting locks and sailing under fixed bridges limits the size of boats that can travel the Great Loop route. This doesn't stop some from purchasing the biggest possible boat to create a floating bacchanalia. Large boats with multiple staterooms and bathrooms, laundry facilities, dishwashers, air conditioning, and satellite entertainment systems give the owners all the comforts of an upper middle-class home. Nothing wrong with that. I have always felt one of the most appealing aspects of life afloat is the difference to my life on land; the realization that a simple life without all the bells and whistles of twenty-first century life can be enjoyable and fulfilling.

We chose a modestly sized boat that we could live on comfortably and that would be seaworthy enough to handle the open water passages.

This book is not a cruising guide or a how-to book about the Great Loop. It is a travel journal compiled by two people with uniquely different perspectives and insights. Jill is a free spirit visual artist, and I am a more pragmatic personality with an interest in navigation and maritime history. Though we shared this journey together each experienced it in our own way. The difference between the shared adventure and the very personal nature of each of our realities is what this book is about.

During our trip I sent email updates called 'voyage logs' to a select group of friends that showed interest in our voyage. These will be inserted into the narrative at the appropriate points. Jill documented our travels with photographs and posts on social media. She also kept a sketch journal. Her photos, artwork, and journal entries will be printed as a counterpoint. We have several artist friends who created artworks to celebrate the adventure. We have included these as well.

Prologue

Mid-September, 2022

I wake up to the sound of the pennant on the bow snapping in the breeze. The nylon bridle squeals as it stretches, and the anchor chain rumbles along the rocky bottom as the boat swings to the wind. Rain patters on the plexiglass hatch above the v-berth. This was not predicted. I fumble for my glasses and the iPhone on the shelf. The weather app screen is a color-coded chart, and the red and orange colors mean wind speeds of 25 to 30 knots in our location. I scroll through the screens and discover winds will only increase as the day progresses. I check the anchor alarm and it shows we are still holding our position, but for how long? This anchorage is pretty exposed with a straight shot to the open Atlantic. When we dropped the hook eight hours ago it was a reasonable spot considering the benign forecast. Now it might be untenable. The wind is from the west giving it many miles of fetch to build waves. How much scope did we use? I suspect we figured 5 to 1 which was reasonable considering the eight knots of winds we were expecting. I need to get up and climb out on the foredeck to let out another thirty feet or so of chain. Jill needs to be part of this. Going out on the deck at night on a boat hobby-horsing in the waves means a possibility of slipping and maybe even being separated from the boat. Having another crew member awake and alert is a standard procedure on the *Alvin James*. I reach over to shake Jill but she's not there! My mind reels. Wait a damn minute. I'm not in a v-berth, I'm in my bed. In a house. Firmly anchored on terra firma. We returned from our yearlong loop over a week ago. Jill is on the far end of our bed sleeping and breathing softly. The night is still.

For the last year I woke up in the early morning hours and obsessively checked weather predictions, the anchor alarm, and the state of the ship's batteries. I reviewed our planned route considering how the latest weather info might affect our plans. Wind speed and direction had huge consequences and could mean the difference between a lovely day on the water and a white knuckled thrill ride. Weather was the big issue, but there were others clustered around the periphery that also required attention. What was the status of our fresh water supply? How full was our waste tank? Where was the opportunity to buy fuel, get a pump out, and get potable water? Now that we are home those are no longer concerns but the muscle memory after a year and eight days afloat persists.

The friends made, the sights seen, and the adventures experienced will always stay with us but the minutia of piloting a small boat thousands of miles will eventually be relegated to that broom closet of our minds that store all those critical but unremarkable events in our lives like washing dishes, cleaning out the garage, or mowing the lawn. It's time to go back to sleep.

From the Great Lakes to the Gulf Coast

A circle is the longest distance to the same point.

Tom Stoppard

We planned to spend the Fall of 2021 traveling south to the Gulf of Mexico, staying one step ahead of Winter's icy embrace. The trip would involve leaving our home in Manitowoc, Wisconsin, and coasting down the shore of Lake Michigan to Chicago before entering the river system and traveling to Mobile Bay. The highlights of the trip would be visits to our old haunts in Milwaukee and Chicago, visiting relatives in Peoria, Illinois, a few days in Paducah, Kentucky, and Fair Hope, Alabama.

I had promised friends that they could expect an email update from me every few weeks with information on our progress. I sent the first of these "Voyage Logs" the day before we left. It is reprinted here:

Voyage Log #1
Friends and Shipmates,

A small boat on a big voyage. This is the motor vessel Alvin James. Named after my father. He was a decent, reliable man. I hope this boat lives up to that name. This Thursday (weather permitting) we will cast off lines and start a circumnavigation of the eastern third of the United States. First leg is down the rivers to the Gulf of Mexico. After wintering in warmer climes we will head north on the Atlantic coast and then be home again next summer.

This trip is known as the Great Loop. About one hundred boats and crews accomplish this each year. To put that into perspective about 26,000 people finish the Boston Marathon, about 1,000 people complete the Appalachian Trail, about

600 climbers reach the summit of Mount Everest, and about 100 swimmers cross the English Channel. Jill and I will let you know how it goes.

Stay safe, stay healthy.

    Because the pandemic was still a reason for concern, I concluded each Voyage Log with the admonition to stay safe and healthy.

    I considered the Lake Michigan leg a kind of shakedown in familiar waters testing our systems before getting too far from home. There were quite a few bits of new equipment we had installed or modified over the off season. New wiring and antenna for our VHF radio. A new navigation system with AIS, a dripless shaft seal, new shower sump pump, and various other improvements. We did have one worrying moment a few miles from Sheboygan when the engine started clattering noticeably louder than normal. Damn! Only fifteen miles from our slip! We slowed down and I lifted the floorboards to peer into the engine compartment. Nothing seemed amiss and when we increased the RPMs the clattering disappeared and did not return when we resumed our normal cruising speed. In Sheboygan I bought an oil and fuel supplement advertised as effective in reducing valve clatter in older engines. I added a bit to the crankcase oil, and the fuel and the clattering was gone for months. Our youngest son lives in Sheboygan, and we had a nice visit. There were several other loop boats in the harbor, and we did some visiting. Of course, Covid still loomed large and we were cautious. Both Jill and I are veterans, and we got our vaccinations through the VA. When meeting people I would enquire about their vaccination status. I was relieved to hear that everyone we met said they had gotten their shots. That evening we decided to dine with some new acquaintances at the Sheboygan Yacht Club. This was a bit of a stretch for us as we hadn't eaten at an indoor restaurant for over a year. We sat at a round table with the crews of two other boats. The conversation was amiable and concerned the various stages of the adventure we were all on. In the course of the evening unknown to me a woman sitting next to Jill confided that she was not vaccinated and had no intention of doing so. Jill excused herself to go to the ladies room. Several minutes later I got a text from Jill saying she was outside and would not be returning. I apologized to my table mates saying that Jill felt a bit ill and would be returning to the boat. I put some money on the table and left. We vowed to be more careful in the future.

Conditions on the big lake were not cooperating and we stayed in port for two more days before leaving under blue skies and calm seas for Milwaukee. Jill and I raised our children in Milwaukee and are very fond of the city. We had reservations for a slip at Lakeshore State Park. The park is a tranquil oasis in the heart of Milwaukee's lakefront. The marina has only twenty-two slips and very little in the way of amenities, but has miles of hiking and biking trails and is a reasonable walk to the Third Ward entertainment and shopping district. We stayed four days and were visited by friends and family that lived nearby.

Our next destination was Chicago. We decided to break the ninety-five-mile passage into two more manageable bites. After fueling up and pumping out at McKinley Marina we motored down the coast to Prairie Harbor Yacht Club. Much of the marina was under construction and was pretty unmemorable with the exception of a heart in your throat entrance through a narrow channel filled with breaking waves.

Arriving the next day in Chicago we had reserved a slip in Burnham Harbor. We spent the next four days enjoying the city. In the course of our stay, we met the crews of several other boats that were planning to leave the same day we had scheduled and thought it was a good idea to coordinate our departure time to make transiting the upcoming locks more efficient.

One of the pitfalls of any trip is discovering the reality of something you had eagerly anticipated fails to live up to those expectations. Leaving Lake Michigan and locking through to the Chicago River and through the heart of the city was something we had looked forward to since we first thought of doing the Great Loop. It did not disappoint. Gliding down the river through a canyon of skyscrapers and under dozens of bridges alive with the bustle of rush hour commuters was as exciting as we had imagined it would be.

The glass and steel magnificence of downtown Chicago abruptly became an industrial corridor lined with moored barges and huge mounds of scrap iron and wood. Towboats prowled the canal hauling or assembling barges for transport downriver. There was a strong petroleum smell in the air and the water looked dark, greasy, and uninviting. It was apparent that this was the rusty, clanking industrial heart of the city that pumped life blood into the land of beautiful skyscrapers and boulevards of Chicago.

It was necessary to communicate by radio with the towboats that seemed to be everywhere. We identified ourselves and asked for instructions on how to pass on the narrow waterway. The captains were unfailingly courteous and helpful, and their advice was delivered with efficient accuracy. Some seemed thankful that we realized we were passing through their working environment and were willing to operate by their rules. The very act of establishing contact with them signalled we were not in that category of clueless pleasure boaters with minimal situational awareness capable of unexpectedly reckless maneuvers that made the jobs of professional watermen more stressful.

Later in the afternoon we arrived at Lockport, Illinois and the first big lock on the river. We had an hour to wait while an upbound tow locked through. During the wait while we slowly circled in the river attempting to hold station near the lock gates, more pleasure boats arrived, many flying AGLCA (America's Great Loop Cruisers' Association) flags. The weather was good and many looper crews that had been waiting in Chicago had decided that today was a good day to start the trek down river. We all moved aside as the gates opened and the tow and its load of barges exited the lock. The lockmaster requested we enter the lock in the order we arrived. The first boats in were instructed to go to the far end of the chamber and tie up on either the port or starboard side. Soon all the available wall space was filled, and the lockmaster asked that later arriving boats raft up to those already on the wall. A large power cruiser about twenty feet longer than the *Alvin James* pulled alongside and asked us to take their lines. We complied but the difference in scale between the boats created problems. The deck of the big boat was about six feet higher than our deck which made it difficult and occasionally impossible to see the crew as they moved closer to tie off. Had the big boat been tied to the wall, we could have easily rafted off to them, but in this situation, we had an enormous boat essentially using our boat as a fender to keep them off the rough, slimy wall. Our fenders were compressed to the maximum, and it seemed that damage was inevitable. Fortunately, the lockmaster became aware of the issue and ordered the bigger boat to untie and move back to a craft of similar size. The rest of the locking procedure was uneventful.

Several miles from the lock was the city of Joliet, Illinois. Joliet has a free wall with electric hook ups and is adjacent to a city park. It is a quiet and pleasant place to spend the night. We decided to spend an additional day and made arrangements to get our groceries delivered by a shopping service the next day,

Leaving Joliet, we traveled with six other looper boats. Most of them were planning to travel about 40 miles to the Heritage Harbor Marina. Our original plan was not to stay at a marina but to anchor out of the channel behind a small island. However, when we arrived low water levels made the entrance an iffy proposition. As the rest of our little flotilla steamed on toward Heritage Harbor a sailboat in our group hung back and tried to assist us in finding a path with sufficient depth to get to the anchorage. The captain launched the dinghy and motored back and forth taking readings with a portable depth finder. No luck. There was a sand bar three feet under water across the entrance. *Alvin James* draws 3½ feet and the sailboat draws five. We contacted the marina, made reservations for slips, and continued on our way. We arrived in the evening and while negotiating the entrance channel our friends on the sailboat hit an underwater obstruction hard enough that they were concerned about the integrity of their hull. It turns out all was well, but it proved once again that a shallow draft is your friend on the Great Loop.

Heritage Harbor Marina is a combination marina and luxury condominium development. Very upscale and comfortable with a swimming pool and restaurants on the premises. We hung out a few days enjoying the pool and hot showers and becoming better acquainted with some of the crews we were traveling with. As pleasant as it was, luxury condo developments are not our idea of the kind of adventure we were seeking. I kept thinking that at any moment we would be accosted by a smarmy salesperson extolling the not to be missed opportunity to purchase a time-share unit.

After fueling up in the morning we left and then after a pleasant day on the water, we anchored at lower Henry Island. A beautiful peaceful night on the river followed.

The next day we traveled to the Illinois Valley Yacht Club, known as the IVY Club. We planned a longer stay here because it is the home of Jill's surviving relatives and Covid protocols had kept us apart for the previous year. We rented a car and took care of chores like shopping and having boat cards made to replace the ones we managed to lose on the boat (on a 33-foot boat!). Of course, we found the misplaced cards not long after. As good a time as we had we were eager to get on the way and continue our trip.

Voyage Log #2
Friends and Shipmates,

When you last heard from me, I was sipping a vodka and tonic poolside at the Heritage Harbor Marina in Ottawa, Illinois. After topping off our fuel tanks and water tanks and pumping out our holding tanks, we motored downriver to an idyllic anchorage behind Lower Henry Island. I knew from conversations with fellow loopers that several boats were planning on anchoring there. They all left at the crack of dawn to get there while Jill and I dawdled at the fuel dock and left several hours after the pack. Speaking of fellow loopers, it is a mixed bag. Everyone we meet seems very nice, but everyone is unique. I am amazed at how many people have sold their homes and moved onto their boats full-time. That's quite a commitment! In fact, Jill and I have been asked numerous times if we still have a "dirt home!" Weird.

When we arrived at the anchorage the four boats that had left before us had already settled in.

We were hailed on the radio and invited to raft up with the group. I thanked them for being so welcoming but (being sailors at heart) dropped anchor alone in order to enjoy the solitude. We were rewarded by a peaceful night with a nearly full moon and a very gentle current that kept us from swinging at anchor.

At 7:00 a.m. we left and headed to the Illinois Valley Yacht and Canoe Club in Peoria, Illinois. This had been a long-anticipated stop because Jill has family here that we have not seen in several years. The water on the river is very low and the entrance to many marinas and fuel docks are too shallow for deep draft boats, and by deep draft I mean five feet! A sailboat traveling with us was running low on fuel and had to launch a dinghy to enter a harbor and bring diesel fuel out to the mother ship in jerry cans. We are fortunate we only draw 3½ feet.

Peoria has gained a reputation over the years for being the dullest city in America. Mark Twain supposedly quipped that he spent four years in Peoria one night. I suspect that wasn't Twain but some vaudeville comedian. My experience is that it is an interesting place with museums, restaurants, and some amazingly picturesque overlooks of the river from the forested hills around town.

We will leave Peoria on Friday and hope to make the confluence of the mighty Mississippi in three days. Shallow water means no more marinas and anchorages with very iffy approaches. Should be pretty challenging but this is an adventure, right?

Stay safe, stay in touch.

The next three nights we anchored out each evening.

Each night is spent off the channel behind a small island. The current is moderate, and the islands shelter us from the wakes of passing towboats. We read, cook dinner, have an after-dinner drink, and are in bed when the sun goes down. This natural sleep cycle is in part required by our need to preserve our batteries which would be stressed if we burned lights late into the evening. We do have a small gas generator, but we are loathe to use it and solar panels keep us charged up when at anchor. The short days of late Fall mean there is less time for the panels to collect energy and long nights to suck energy out of the battery banks. The refrigerator and freezer are the big draw but lights and radio also have a cumulative effect on our system. Conservation is our watchword.

The river seems to alternate from areas crowded with industrial activity and long stretches of undeveloped areas where the impact of human activity is all but undetectable. These areas create a slow hypnotic beauty as the river slowly meanders between forested banks teeming with waterfowl, turtles, and aquatic mammals. In the evenings deer are often seen.

On our fourth day after leaving Peoria we arrive in Grafton, Illinois where the Illinois River empties into the Mississippi. Grafton promotes itself as the "Key West of the Midwest." Having lived in the Florida Keys and worked in Key West I struggle to see the similarities. Grafton has some fun waterfront bars and restaurants, but it lacks the vibrant social gumbo made of Cuban and Bahamian influences, an open acceptance of gay culture, and historic neighborhoods filled with uniquely Caribbean homes, art galleries, and a long literary tradition. I would rate Grafton as a town that is worth a stop but Key West it is not.

Stay safe, stay in touch.

Voyage Log #3
Friends and Shipmates,

Today, Sunday the 26th of September, we transited the last of eight locks on the Illinois River. Tonight, we are anchored in the lee of Wing Island about 40 miles from Grafton, Illinois, and the confluence of the Mississippi River. The Mississippi has loomed large in my thoughts for a while with its fast current, monster tows, and boat-wrecking debris to look out for. The "Father of Waters" is a challenge, but I am ready for the mother of all battles with the big river.

Grafton is supposed to be a nice town to hang out and provision in. It labels itself as the "Key West of the Midwest." Maybe, maybe not. I'll let you know. I can't be too snarky since I often jokingly refer to my hometown of Manitowoc, WI as the "Paris of the Midwest." Jill and I are looking forward to getting off the boat and eating in an outdoor café. Also on the agenda is ridding the boat of spiders and their ever- present detritus.

Some loopers seem to travel in packs, sometimes with as many as a dozen boats. Jill and I are very social, but we enjoy being the only boat in an anchorage. We limit our travel time to about six hours a day and try to tuck into a peaceful cove in time to relax and read (or nap). Then at about five, it's time for a relaxing drink before preparing the evening meal. Dinner on the boat is always an event I enjoy. Jill is not only co-captain but the creative cook and communication director on the Alvin James. We are a good team and so far, things are going well.

Stay healthy and stay in touch.

Next stop was Alton, Illinois. This river town has seen better days, but it seems there is an effort to come back. In the evening there was an art gallery tour with a free shuttle service. The following evening a captain's meeting was organized so crews could coordinate departure times and be more efficient transiting the locks. One captain with lots of river experience volunteered to be the point person of our group and communicate with the locks. A phone conversation with the Melvin Price Lock revealed that if our flotilla of pleasure boats could assemble in front of the lock at 8:00 a.m. we would be locked through. Since the lock was only about a half mile from the marina it was decided that leaving at 7:30 a.m. would give us plenty of time. It was agreed that communication between boats would be on VHF Channel 68 and our point person would talk to the lockmaster on VHF Channel 14.

Our plan, which had been laid out with military precision, ran into a snag almost immediately. As we approached the lock, we were informed that an upbound tow was entering the lock and would delay us about an hour. Well, there wasn't any suitable alternative, so we cruised in lazy circles, killing time, until it was our turn. A fact of life on the rivers is that commercial and military traffic has priority. Pleasure boats or 'rec-boats' (short for recreational boats) must wait. If there are enough rec-boats to fill his lock chamber most lockmasters will try to fit them in between tows. This is why it is advisable to travel in a pack on the rivers.

The next lock was the Chain of Rocks Lock and Dam. Nothing particularly noteworthy and after about another hour's wait, we managed to get through. However, a mile or so before approaching the lock the boater has a choice;

Photo credit: Joe Clark

Alvin James passing the Gateway Arch

there is a narrow canal to port and the river continues to starboard. The canal is the only safe route. Following the river to starboard leads you to the Chain of Rocks rapids and almost certain catastrophe. There is a sign, too small some say considering the result of a poor decision, warning boats to keep left. Later that very same day a big sailboat did exactly that and was wrecked on the Chain of Rocks. The crew was rescued by a coast guard helicopter but before salvage operations could be arranged, the boat, its hull holed by the rocks, was swept into deeper water, and disappeared never to be seen again.

After the Chain of Rocks lock, we glided past St. Louis and its iconic Gateway Arch. It is a spectacular piece of architecture by Eero Sarrinen and of course it's a great photo opportunity. We were fortunate that one of our friends on another boat offered to photograph us as we steamed past the arch. It was a beautiful clear Fall day and the sun was in the perfect position to illuminate the arch and the *Alvin James*. Jill and I felt we had achieved another milestone on our journey. St. Louis surprisingly has no facilities for the recreational boater. The river has such a fast current, and fluctuations in the water level would make building a marina technically challenging and god-awful expensive, so we just motored past and headed for the legendary Hoppies Marina. Now Hoppies is legendary for a couple of reasons. One is that it is the last fuel stop for a couple hundred miles. Two is that the 85-year proprietor, Fern Hoppie, is very knowledgeable about this stretch of the Mississippi. She talks to all the tow captains on the radio and gets up-to-date information on shallow water, obstructions, or any other issues that a traveler might need to know. The marina is a minimal affair, just a string of barges cabled to the riverbank, but the availability of fuel and Fern's daily briefing make it wildly popular with boats traversing this section of the river.

We tried to make reservations but were told that they were full. Studying the charts, I noticed there was a wing dam just south of Hoppies that had sufficient depth to anchor behind it, and we decided that was where we would spend the night. We dropped the hook about 50 yards from the wing dam in six feet of water. There was very little discernible current, and the dam protected us from towboat wakes and debris floating down river. A sailboat soon joined us and promptly ran aground while backing down from their anchor. They were not able to power their way off and were not able to retrieve their anchor. They did not have a windlass and were not able to muscle it up by hand. Jill and I launched our dinghy and trouble shot with the sailboat crew, eventually sorting things out and getting them floating again and re-anchored.

The low water on the river made some anchorages we had considered too shallow to enter, so the following night we just pulled out of the marked channel and spent the night. Our next real anchorage was Little Diversion Channel and water levels made it tighter than it looked on the charts, but we nosed up a narrow creek about 100 yards and dropped anchor in about four feet of water.

Later that evening, some recent friends on the Trawler 'Holly Grove' came in and rafted to us. It was a snug fit, but it was nice to have company.

The next day we made it to Boston Bar, the last anchorage before leaving the Mississippi and turning onto the Ohio.

Voyage Log #4
Friends and Shipmates,

It's October 4th and the Alvin James is anchored along the banks of the Mississippi about 20 miles south of St. Louis. We are tucked in between two wing dams that provide some protection from the debris that flows downstream in the current. Yesterday we left Alton, Illinois, transited two locks with an hour-plus wait at each one. Those are the last locks we will need to pass through until we reach the Ohio River.

A bit of drama in the anchorage. A sailboat with a young family radioed and asked if there was room for another boat. I responded that there was and that there was about 10 feet of depth between the dams. They came in and thought it might be a good idea to snuggle up close to the dam and drop anchor. When they backed down to set the hook, they ran aground in hard sand. Not only were they aground, but they couldn't retrieve the anchor! They radioed for help, and Jill and I launched our dinghy. I motored over to see what I could do. First, we put a chain hook on the anchor chain as low as we could reach in the water. Then we ran the nylon line from the chain hook to a winch on his boat. He was able to winch the anchor out of the water. We put the anchor onto my dinghy and motored out about 200 feet from the boat and in a direction that led to deeper water.

With much effort cranking the winch, he was able to pull his boat off the sandbar and was afloat once more. As they began to anchor again in a more suitable place, I went back to Alvin James where Jill and I stowed the dinghy and had a drink. We had done our good deed, and we slept the sleep of the just.

We have three more days on the Mississippi before we turn on the Ohio River and stop for several days at Paducah, Kentucky. This stretch of the Mississippi is surprisingly remote with only one marina and no places to buy fuel. As far as anchorages, we put down our anchor anywhere we can find with enough water under our keel and far enough out of the channel so we won't be run down by the tows. We have seen no pleasure boats (except for a few loopers; and just a few fishing boats and many working vessels. This is not like Florida.

Though I am usually occupied with captainy stuff, I still have time to appreciate the beauty of the rivers and the fact that I am fortunate enough to share this with my best friend.

Stay safe, stay in touch.

The confluence of the Ohio River and the Mississippi at Cairo, Illinois was filled with barges. I had never seen so many barges. Some were anchored seemingly mid-channel while others lined the shores three or four deep. Towboats scurried about assembling individual barges into massive rafts numbering fifteen or more. Adding to my disorientation was the fact the current of the Ohio was against us after several hundred miles being assisted by the Mississippi's powerful flow. Our speed on the Mississippi averaged close to nine knots while the engine loafed along at about 1300 RPMs. Now with the diesel turning at 2200 RPMs our speed barely topped 4 knots. The 54-mile trip to Paducah, Kentucky promised to be a long day. Already concerned about our arrival time at Paducah we encountered a four-hour delay at the Olmsted Lock! Barge traffic was backed up in both directions and of course we were in the lowest priority group. After motoring around in the current for an hour a tow captain took mercy on us and said that all the rec-boats could tie off on his barges to wait for an opening. We thanked him profusely and we were a grateful group of boaters when hours later the lockmaster announced we could lock through.

Now the race was on. It looked very unlikely that the slower boats (like us) could make it to the marina before dark. Navigating on the river at night was not an appealing prospect. Some crews made a decision to find a spot to anchor before the sun went down. Jill and I decided to push on all the way to Paducah. Our friends on *Holly Grove* had arrived yesterday and texted us that although the dock was full, we could raft up to them. The fast boats disappeared in the distance throwing up huge wakes and traveling at speeds over 20 knots. Jill and I plowed ahead against the current as the sun dropped like a ball towards the horizon. When the sun dropped below the tree line daylight turned to dusk and we were still miles from our destination. Soon dusk became the blackest night and we struggled to spot the navigation markers we required to keep us safely in the channel. Soon some faint lights on a distant shore coincided with the location of the marina on our chart plotter. We contacted *Holly Grove* on the radio and requested they get ready to take our lines. Soon we were tied up and were looking forward to spending several days not moving the boat and enjoying the little city of Paducah.

The captain of one of the fast boats walked over and mentioned that he made it from the Olmstead Lock in only two hours. He also mentioned that in that 35-mile jaunt he burned over 30 gallons of diesel fuel per hour! I later thought to myself that six years ago I had sailed a 37-foot boat from Norfolk, Virginia to Lagos, Portugal and probably burned less fuel.

The next several days were spent exploring Paducah's many treasures. The National Quilt Museum is a place to see great works of imagination and examples of jaw-dropping virtuosity. The Concrete flood wall which was erected by the city to protect the town from catastrophic flooding is home to a series of beautifully rendered historic murals that tell the story of the Indigenous inhabitants and the development of the city into a commercial and cultural center on the river.

After Paducah Loopers leave the Ohio River and continue south to the Gulf on the Tennessee River. The most direct route is to turn on to the Tennessee River just a mile past Paducah. A less direct and longer route is to continue on the Ohio to the Cumberland River and follow its winding course to the Tennessee River. Both routes have you ending up in the same place. The direct and shorter route often takes longer due to commercial congestion at the Kentucky Lake Lock and Dam. The Cumberland River route is often more trouble free because of the sparse traffic and the resulting shorter waiting times at the Barkley Lake Lock and Dam. Once again because of the lock transits a captains' meeting was called to coordinate activities. Discussions with the lockmaster informed us that in order to prevent flooding upriver in Nashville the dam was releasing over 80,000 gallons of water per second, creating a very strong current on the Cumberland. The Tennessee lock reported that traffic volume was higher than usual and lengthy delays should be expected. The consensus was to go the Cumberland route, current be damned! Early next morning our little fleet left the dock and powered up the Ohio to the Cumberland and started our long slow trek against a raging current. Some parts of the river had the appearance of rapids with rips and boils covering the surface. We ran the engine at 2400 RPMs and still our speed often dipped to about three knots. Tree limbs and sometimes whole trees rushed down river along with various other bits of flotsam and needed a careful watch and fast reflexes to avoid. But avoid them we did, and we were rewarded with a no-wait passage through the Barkley Lock and into tranquil Lake Barkley and a scheduled stay at the Green Turtle Marina. We hung out at the Green Turtle Marina for a bit of socializing with friends old and new. I changed the oil and filters, and Jill bought a fishing license for the promised fishing bonanza that awaited us in the coves and bays of Kentucky Lake.

Voyage Log #5
Friends and Shipmates,

Friday October 15th finds the Alvin James tucked into a slip at the Green Turtle Marina on the Cumberland River in the state of Kentucky. Since the last report we have cruised down the Mississippi River to Cairo, Illinois. From there we fought the current of the Ohio River to Paducah, Kentucky. Leaving Paducah, we traveled farther up the Ohio River to the Cumberland River and through the Barkley Lock. There, the river widens into Lake Barkley, where the marina is located. A rest was in order, so we decided to stay for seven days. Time is spent reprovisioning, cleaning, changing oil and filters, taking hot showers, and enjoying general R&R before the trip down to the Gulf.

The Mississippi River was not the horror show that existed in my imagination. Challenging for sure, but nothing unmanageable. We anchored out every night and actually spent five days without getting off the boat.

Turning onto the Ohio River, we lost the favorable current of the Mississippi and pushed our way against a powerful current that slowed us down and caused us to burn more fuel. Our destination for the day was Paducah, Kentucky. At a distance of 49 miles, it seemed an early start would put us in Paducah in daylight. However, my careful navigation was undone by a four-hour delay at the Olmstead Lock. We had collected a group of eight pleasure boats in the course of the day and we all arrived at the lock requesting transit. Unfortunately, for us, there were also several commercial tows looking for transit in each direction. Since pleasure boats are the lowest priority. We maneuvered against the current trying to stay in place. After an hour or so, a towboat captain took pity on us and invited us to tie up to his string of barges that were resting against the riverbank. It was a great relief to tie up, turn off the engines and wait in relative peace. About three hours later the lockmaster gave us permission to lock through. Now it was a race to get to the docks in Paducah before darkness set in. The fast boats took off and several of the slower boats decided to find an anchorage before dark. Jill and I, after much consideration, decided to try for Paducah before it got too dark. We almost made it. The sun set while we were about one hour away, and it was pitch black by the time we arrived. Some friends on another boat invited us to raft up to them and then made us a spaghetti dinner! To have a long arduous day and be rewarded with a home-cooked meal was truly a kindness I shall not soon forget.

We stayed three days in Paducah, and it is a very charming city. A very charming city with a beautiful downtown and wonderful restaurants, art galleries, and a museum. We will return to visit (by car) after this adventure is over.

The final leg before arriving in our present location was a 40-mile trip up the Cumberland River. The lockmaster at the Barkley Lock on the Cumberland warned us that they were releasing 80,000 gallons of water per second into the Cumberland to prevent flooding upriver in Nashville. The result was a ferocious 5-knot current that turned the surface of the river into a chaotic riot of swirls, eddies, and rips. Sometimes the boat's speed fell below three knots as we battled our way upstream. Logs speeding downstream created an obstacle course that kept us alert. One of the faster boats that passed us early on suffered serious prop and strut damage but managed to limp into the marina.

So here we are, getting ready to travel through Kentucky, Tennessee, Alabama, and Mississippi on our way south.

Stay well my friends.
Let's all stay in touch.

Needing a break from traveling in a pack from lock to lock, Jill and I left on our own and anchored in Pisgah Bay. We launched the dinghy and trolled along the shoreline. We got several bites and Jill caught a couple of bass. They were of a decent size, but we threw them back because we knew that larger fish were waiting for us to arrive. Well, we never caught another fish until we got to Canada, 10 months later! The next night we traveled to Sugar Bay without even a nibble. We knew the legendary fishing reputation of this area must have a basis in fact, but we just didn't know where to find them. The weather was beginning to turn cold, so we decided to put the fishing gear away and concentrate on heading south and staying ahead of the encroaching winter.

The next three and a half weeks were spent cruising south on the Tennessee-Tombigbee Waterway. This is a two-hundred-mile man-made waterway that connects the Tennessee River to the Tombigbee River system. We stayed at quaint rural marinas and anchored in oxbows behind islands. The prices at marinas were the least expensive we had seen, and the people were very welcoming and curious about our trip.

I had planned our next stop to be a nice marina at Pebble Isle. It was reportedly very picturesque and part of an extensive and popular state park. We were on our way when I noticed the name of the park: Nathan Bedford Forrest State Park. Yes, it turns out that Tennessee decided to name one of its state parks after a Confederate general accused of the massacre of hundreds of surrendering Black Union soldiers. Oh, and another thing; he was the very first Grand Wizard of the Ku Klux Klan!

I just couldn't bear the thought of paying any fee to a state park honoring such an odious character, so Jill and I motored about 20 miles farther to the rustic Cuba Landing Marina.

At Cuba Landing Marina a very friendly, somewhat inebriated woman with rainbow dyed hair offered us her car and insisted we have dinner at a local restaurant she said we should not miss. When we hesitated, saying we might just stay on the boat, she insisted and repeated that this restaurant was not to be missed! We could not refuse. She gave us directions and the keys to her car. She was right. The place was charming and served traditional Southern fare and was one of the gastronomical highlights of the trip. A man at the same marina named Roger Miller, (yes, that's his real name!) who lived on his boat introduced himself and turned out to be an exceptional raconteur. He kept us entertained with tales of local lore. He seemed to know everyone of any note in this part of the state; every sheriff, politician, well digger, diesel mechanic, marina manager, school principal, restaurant owner, and every rascal and scoundrel on the river. He was a wealth of information. A day later we had traveled down the river about 40 miles to another marina and he recognized our boat while driving by in his truck. He stopped and walked over to our boat just to say hello. We spent an hour or so sitting on the back deck of the *Alvin James* swapping stories and enjoying each other's company.

The farther south we traveled the more the river twisted and turned back on itself in sinuous lazy arcs. Some days fifty miles of traveling only resulted in 20 miles towards our destination. Traveling on the river was an exercise in patience. Those Type A captains who spent their careers in corporate America always seeking the fastest most efficient paths to accomplish goals were slowly going mad. The conversations at happy hour saw them cursing the rivers with their twists and turns and unexpected delays at locks. They could not wait to be done with this part of the voyage.

I feel foolish admitting this, but I never factored into my solar energy equations that the shorter days in fall would translate into less solar energy collected. Since all my boating on the Great Lakes is in the summer, I could always count on many hours of sunlight. Not so much now when it is still dark at 6:00 a.m. and is dark again by 6:00 p.m. So, after a day or two at anchor, I have to burn fossil fuel to top off the batteries.

The rivers were often blanketed in early morning fog, and we would wait an hour or so for it to burn off before continuing. The shores became more tropical with palms and other vegetation growing right on the edges. Some crews reported alligator sightings but as alert as we were we never saw any. We transited the Coffeeville Lock and celebrated the fact that it was our last lock for over a thousand miles. Then suddenly the river opened up to the port of Mobile, busy with all manner of shipping and then widened into Mobile Bay itself, ten miles wide and a view of the limitless horizon of the Gulf of Mexico. Our river journey was at an end: we were in the salt water of the Atlantic Ocean.

Excerpts from Jill's Sketch Journal:
The Rivers

9/3 After many days of preparation, the boat is loaded, we have said our goodbyes, and we are on our way. This year away from home means life will be different. I need to step aside from so many people and activities I enjoy. It also offers new opportunities. My art practice will have to look different because I won't have a brick-and-mortar art studio to do mosaics and print making. But creative time is my goal, and we've chosen a drawer on Alvin James for art supplies and I am committed to use part of every day for creative practice. So, in my

drawer I have pencils, pens, paper sketch books, embroidery supplies, and collage tools. The size of my drawer forces simplicity. On my first day I split the page into six squares, and I was off...this approach seemed easier than starting with a big blank page.

The loop is about arranging to spend a large chunk of time alone, with no particular goal besides moving on - no news, or keeping track of this and that. Just my time at the helm, sketch journal, and basic needs to take care of: food, comfort, and survival. There is an economy and urgency to life and in place of the usual clutter there is daylight and darkness, and joy and fear.

9/10 Approaching Chicago - Seeing the skyline from the (calm) waters for the first time was exciting. Though we met here, and lived here in our early years, this is a new perspective and Chicago looks wonderful, and feels like home.

9/11 Burnham Harbor is close enough for exploring the city and has great views of the skyline. From the aft deck I sketched the windows which were strategically lit to spell out "NEVER FORGET."

9/13 This morning I woke up feeling excited and a little nervous about transiting our first lock. I had my gloves and knife handy and was ready. I told the lockmaster that it was our first lock, and he shared some tips. It was fine. Moving down the Chicago River in the early morning was dramatic and beautiful. Though we were the only boat on the river there was so much bustle on shore as people made their way to work. Besides the amazing architecture I enjoyed seeing large public art and all the sounds and sights of the city waking up. What a great way to start the Great Loop!

9/13 Joliet - Pelicans, swans, and a cotton mouth snake in the lock. Lots of turtles basking in the sun, a great gray heron, a great white heron, and bright blue darting Kingfishers. Other unknown birds. Bird heaven. The temperature is perfect today.

9/15 Reading "Life at Seven 7 mph" and "The Ditch." They offer lots of useful information. I downloaded the NEBO boater's app and find it to be very helpful. The new habit of starting each cruising day by turning on the app and stopping it when we dock or anchor has begun. It's helpful to know where other loopers are. It tracks our cruising days and our friends can use it to follow us. We enjoyed some days in Heritage Harbor Marina. Met other loopers:

Joe and Kayla are 30-year-olds traveling on a sailboat with a toddler, a dog, and two cats.

Ceci and Tom on the powerboat "Godspeed."

Rob and Robin on "Liberty Call."

It's a challenge to be friendly but keep the right balance because we like our alone time too. Swimming pool is appreciated as a 90-degree heat wave means finding ways to cool down in the hottest part of the day. We have never had air conditioning in our boats or homes, so we are good at finding strategies.

9/18 On our way to Peoria, Illinois to visit with my aunt and uncle. Saw a flock of white domestic geese, unsure of type, emdens? It's too early for the snow geese migration. Also saw my first eagles. We are 310 miles from home now!

9/19 Really enjoyed the historic IVY Club (Illinois Valley Yacht and Canoe Club), and seeing family - probably the last folks from our land lives - another "We are doing this!" step.

Today a 45-ft power yacht came into the cramped marina harbor, at the IVY Club, in a stiff breeze. The man at the helm was having lots of challenges bringing the boat to the dock and several boaters were shouting suggestions to him. I felt nervous for him and felt relieved when he got safely tied up. I met him a bit later when he was wringing his hands on the dock. I said "hello" and Greg introduced himself. He also said, "I bought this boat after only having piloted a small boat. The salesman didn't tell me it might be harder to dock! My wife wanted a big enough boat for her wicker furniture on the aft deck and wouldn't look at anything under 45 feet. We got a good price until I had to do so much repair work. I want to sell the damn thing!" I would learn that Karen and Greg were both very stressed out. Big boat / little experience can be a dangerous combination, and this was just the first of several we would meet in this situation. I hoped they would be OK, but I was concerned. The couple would stick with the loop and succeed, finishing the loop and also becoming our good friends.

We also met the crew of "S.L.O. Dancer" Gary and Annie: a couple in their 80s, spry and positive. We would go on to bump into these folks often on the rivers and get to know each other better each stop. Gary was a seasoned sailor and Annie was working hard to learn to be a good crew member. Annie from S.L.O. Dancer, came and spent a couple of hours with me on the aft deck. She had a huge smile and was charming. She was journaling her loop her way, with photos, found printed materials, and memories. I gave her some peaches and tomatoes, and she gave me some stickers for my journal. She and Gary would become very good friends of ours. We met a lot of Loopers that we were so fond of. Here are some that we really clicked with.

    California - S.L.O. Dancer - Gary & Annie
    Canada/Mexico - Holly Grove - John & Lisa
    Portland, Maine - Sabot - Justin, Melanie, & Peggy
    Virginia - Blue Dreamer - Greg & Karen
    Colorado - Andie Bo - Chuck & Marie
    Maryland/New Jersey - Sweet Day - Kate & Tim

Loopers We Loved - #1

So much love!   Kissing in the locks!

Lisa Reyes + husband John Gannon on MV Holly Grove. She was from Victoria, BC via Philippines - he was from State of Washington. Newly weds - a "covid marriage" (so they could cross borders + be together) who met in Mexico. The 4 of us had lots of laughs + supported each other traveling down the rivers.

We met in Grafton, IL. - introduced by Annie on MV SLO DANCER. Our first dinners out were with MV BLUE DREAMERS, MV SLO DANCER + MV Holly Grove + MV ALVIN James. We buddy-boated + rafted up with Holly Grove several times along the rivers to the Gulf & Mexico. In Florida they sold MV Holly Grove + bought an RV to do road trips. Lisa made me laugh - so funny. We grew quite close.

The river part of the loop we called our "First Family" of friends. We bumped into each other often in locks and marinas - so we had many common bonding experiences.

There is not one way to do the loop. Some are comfortable "Buddy boating" and some prefer more solo cruising. Some prefer marinas to anchoring out. Some need larger living spaces and some like more economical simple spaces.

We enjoyed some buddy boating on the rivers with Holly Grove. We moved at the same speed and rafted up together several times when space was limited, and just to help each other out. We really enjoyed their personalities too,

Especially Lisa, a Canadian of Filipino descent with a great sense of humor. She and John were newlyweds. I sketched them in the locks sharing some love. First in a series I called "Loopers we loved."

9/25 Life on the river means we are migrating with white pelicans, and I am enamored with them. Bar Island anchorage might be the prettiest one so far. Just before we anchored for the night a tug passed us and called us up on the VHS radio to invite us to tie up on their barge the Langston Tug Company. "There is a carnival tonight," he said. We took a pass, chasing the solitude of a free anchorage and I made a nice dinner of Italian Sausage, and peppers on pasta. Very peaceful night of recharging.

9/26 I am getting comfortable conversing with towboat captains, enjoying the brevity and courtesy of the communication on the VHF radio. This morning coming off anchor I saw a tow with a six-pack (a whole bunch of barges) coming down the channel. As I looked at the AIS, I called him up:

Me: "Toulant, Toulant, this is the pleasure vessel Alvin James just in front of you. How might I proceed?"

Him: "Come on the one whistle, Keep coming," delivered with a warm Cajun accent.

Me: "See you on the port side."

Jill holding large wood block print she embroidered along the way.

Him: "Appreciate you calling me up. There's nothing coming up behind me."

Me: "I appreciate you."

As we passed, I saw two people watching us from the high pilothouse with binoculars. We each waved enthusiastically.

9/27 I feel that I am really feeling connected to the rivers, I especially enjoy the wooded sections. I did some stitching on my fabric goose between my turns at the helm. Last night I slept like 10 hours at anchor. In the middle of the night, I awoke to listen to an owl hooting somewhere nearby. Magical! I drifted right back to sleep.

10/8 Paducah, Kentucky - Was a highlight stop so we lingered a few days. The high-water mark on a gorgeous old downtown building gave me a strong image of water over the top of the door frames during a flood year. Astounding. Exploring river culture was very interesting. I also loved learning about the "artist relocation program" and enjoyed masking up and visiting five different gallery/studios in stately renovated homes. We plan to return and spend more time in this place. Paducah is also home of the National Quilt Museum, which we toured with the crews of S.L.O. Dancer and Blue Dreamer.

10/13 Kentucky Lake was on my short list of places I wanted to linger, because I had fished and vacationed there as a child.

Meeting Dave and Sharlot, who travel the rivers on a vintage Carver powerboat named Charlie, and hearing Dave's stories of being present for the flooding of Lake Barkley was fascinating. Dave and Sharlot were boating from Evansville, Indiana. They had lots of local knowledge of the rivers; a couple of the many very special boaters and local people we met who touched our hearts.

On the shore of Green Turtle Beach, I saw a shiny brown thing stuck in the mud and decided to dig it up. It was a vintage doorknob made of porcelain! This sent me off on more imagining about the people who lived in the houses and farms that would be flooded when the river was dammed. These types of knobs were manufactured in the last century. Who turned this knob? How did they feel when their homestead was flooded? My already tightly packed art drawer would be packed and re-packed as I found small mementos like the porcelain doorknob and some shell and bone fragments which I could imagine using in future mosaics. I knew I had to be very selective, keeping very little aboard our small home.

10/23 Local people offered great hospitality and kindness and asked for nothing in return. For instance, Roger Miller and Sharon on the dock at Cuba Landing Marina, brought us laughter, good advice, and the use of a vehicle to eat at the amazing Log Cabin Restaurant! After some years of being a politically divided country, it did our hearts and minds so much good to meet caring people all along our loop.

10/24 Home: It is your sanctuary, your safe nest. But home needn't have four walls to be a nest. Our home expanded as far as we could see and beyond, without boundaries. Our home moved down the Tombigbee Waterway, and because the helm was right next to the galley, I was so satisfied making a delicious stew while motoring down the river and transiting four locks.

10/26 So many new vocabulary words: River Stuff - I feel like every day brings new things to learn. Almost every day I found a few minutes to record what I was thinking, feeling, or experiencing. I rarely had a plan when I opened my art drawer, it just happened.

11/7 We are anchored in a channel ditch behind the Howell Heflin Lock at mm 266. Resting after supper with Channel 13 turned on, we overheard a 5-minute conversation between a towboat captain and the lockmaster. They obviously knew each other well.

"Have you ever seen so many rec-boats? Given the cost of fuel, I hope they're having a fun time." They went on to discuss the cost of roof replacement after a recent tornado, price gouging, the loss of an RV, and it's replacement by insurance...and many other topics. Especially heart-warming was the lockmaster

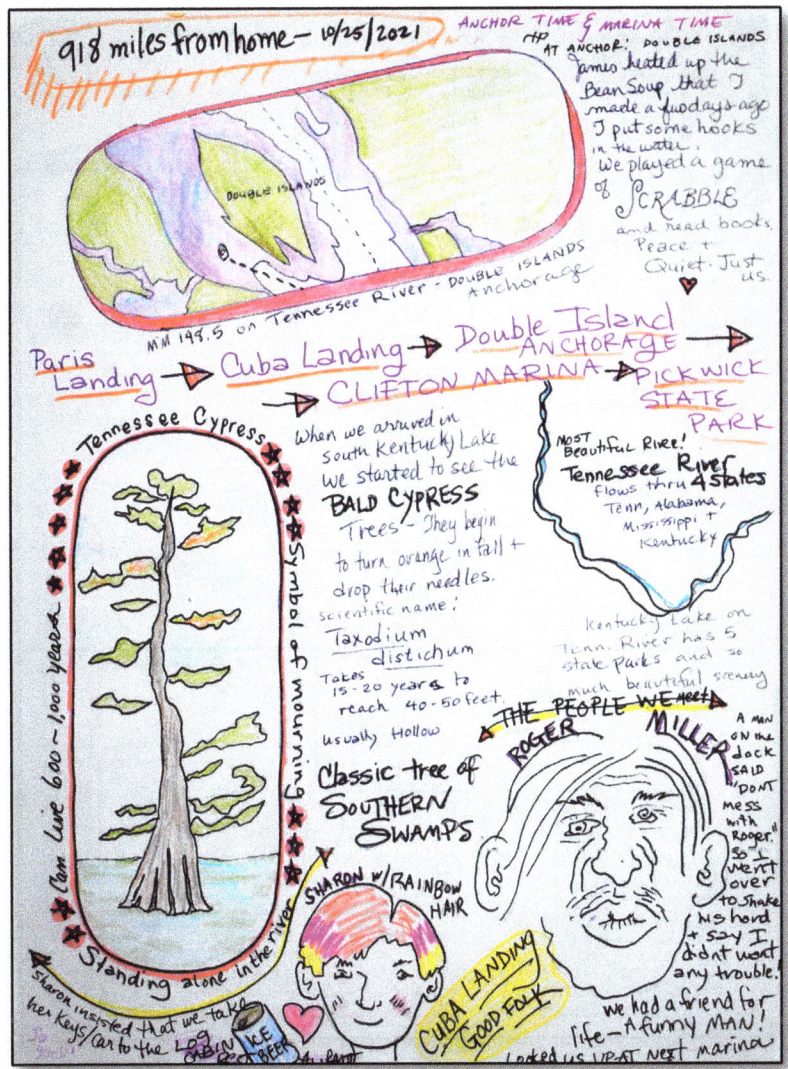

telling the tow captain that he had just received a call from a rec-boat looking for an anchorage in the darkness so they could transit the lock in the morning. "So just watch out for them." I had the sense that they were really caring guys.

11/8 I awoke in the morning remembering a retreat I attended when I was about to turn 50. I thought about how meaningful it is now that I am living it:

"May we live our lives as the river flows...carried by the surprise of its own unfolding." Though not exact this was my memory of John O'Donohue's quote.

11/10 Anchored in a pretty little cove with Holly Grove and a small sailboat piloted by returning veteran Ray T. Sitting on the aft deck in pitch blackness I watched as a towboat swept his spotlight on the shore as he moved at a snail's pace through the darkness. I was amazed that the tows never stopped, running through the night along the narrow channels and around the serpentine curves of the river. So still - so eerie

11/11 Bobby's Fish Camp. It's so rustic. It's the only stop for fuel or to tie up for many miles, in a place where there is not much safe anchoring. It's a hoot! Randal, the owner, stopped to tell us stories as we were having Happy Hour with several looper crews. In his gentle Cajun accent, he told the story of a wom-

an who stopped for fuel one day. "She had a horrible East Coast accent," he said. What a great melding of cultures. We rafted up with Holly Grove at the fish camp's tiny dock. They had a delightful shower converted from a plastic lawn shed! That shower felt so good after many miles of travel!

As we came to the end of our river segment, I decided that someday I would find undredged, unaltered, rivers to quietly kayak down. To see undisturbed wildlife and vegetation. It's also good to see what we humans have done to our lands and rivers. I saw many places where people were doing what they could to restore our waterways.

Holly Grove anchored at night, illuminated by the powerful spotlight of an approaching tow.

The Gulf Coast and Florida

"I would like to travel the world with you twice. Once, to see the world. Twice, to see the way you see the world."

Anonymous

Voyage Log #7
Friends and Shipmates,

On Sunday, November 14,[th] the Alvin James left the rivers and entered the waters of the Gulf of Mexico. We have bisected the country from north to south. It is a milestone that deserves a celebration. We left Demopolis, Alabama, five days ago and transited the last lock for a thousand miles. We will spend a few days at the Grand Mariners Marina on the western shore of Mobile Bay just to decompress before crossing the bay to the eastern shore and spending a week at what is reputed to be the very charming community of Fairhope, Alabama. The city has art galleries, interesting little shops, and great restaurants featuring the seafood the Gulf Coast is famous for. Leaving a wilderness anchorage in the morning and two hours later entering one of the busiest seaports in the United States was awesome. Large container ships and giant car carriers from Asia lined both sides of the port. Futuristic Navy vessels were in dry docks getting maintenance. Tugs and barges were everywhere. Your captain was scolded by a towboat captain who thought my approach was too close. I thought I was keeping a prudent distance, but he disagreed. So, I apologized and wished him a good day. The bay was alive with pelicans and dolphins as well as commercial traffic.

Mobile Bay is a very large body of water, but it is very shallow outside of the dredged channels used by ships. You can find yourself ten miles offshore and be in five feet of water! Close attention to charts and the depth sounder is necessary when under-way.

Besides a week or so of R&R, there are some boat issues that need attention. There is a leak in the pressure water system and the wash down pump has quit working. I also need to change the oil and change the fuel filters. The next leg of our trip, we will be traveling east through the panhandle of Florida. We may also spend some time at the Pensacola Air Force Base Marina. Since my sweetie is a Service-connected Disabled Veteran, we are allowed to stay there at a price substantially lower than other area marinas.

I'll keep you informed as we keep making progress on our journey to complete America's Great Loop.

In the huge estuary of Mobile Bay, we saw our first dolphins, an introduction to the sea life that would make this leg of our journey memorable. We had reservations at the Grand Mariner Marina, where we reconnected with several boats that had accompanied us on the rivers. People doing the loop in sailboats had their masts shipped here and were planning on becoming sailboats again for the trip to the Florida Keys and over to the Bahamas. Our plan was to rest up for a few days and then cross the Bay to Fairhope, Alabama. We had heard that Fairhope was a sophisticated small city that offered gourmet food and a lively street scene. I also planned to do some routine engine maintenance that included changing the fuel filters. Several of our friends were there but they were eager to move on and only stayed one day.

That evening, after wishing the crew of *Holly Grove* farewell, we were walking back to our boat when a car pulled up next to us and asked if we needed a ride. It turned out they were fellow loopers and their boat was tied up on the wall in front of us. We declined because it was such a pleasant evening for strolling along the waterfront. The driver then mentioned that this was a rental car they had for another day, and would we like to accompany them to a grocery store in the morning? We said yes, we would, and arrangements were made to meet at their boat at 9:00 a.m. the following day.

That day we shopped, had a restaurant meal, and all four of us got our Covid booster shots at a local drugstore. A bonding experience! Their boat was named *Sabot*, and they had a wonderful big black lab named Peggy. We planned to spend some time cruising the gulf coast together. They departed the following morning while we stayed an extra day hoping to take care of some issues. When I changed the fuel filters, an air leak was introduced into the lines that I was unable to find and correct. Locating a diesel mechanic on short notice was difficult but we did find one and he arrived the next morning. After two hours of fruitless investigation, we discovered that the culprit was an aftermarket filter I had purchased at an auto supply store. A new filter solved the problem and we planned to leave Fairhope in the morning.

The day dawned gray and blustery as we nosed out of the marina into the wide-open bay. It was lumpy and looked more ominous than it felt as we bashed our way to the entrance of the Gulf Intracoastal Waterway. Once off the bay with its wind-tossed waves, things settled into smooth water in the river-like environs of the GICW. That night we dropped anchor in Ingram Bayou.

It was a wilderness anchorage with no sign of human habitation. We cooked dinner and watched a pod of dolphins feeding in the shallows. Over morning coffee, the dolphins joined us again cooperatively herding and feeding on schools of fish.

Continuing our voyage, we received a text from the crew of *Sabot* mentioning they had been anchored not far from us and suggested we share an anchorage that evening. We agreed and continued west. We were traveling almost a knot faster than *Sabot* and within a few hours we were able to see them ahead of us. Both crews consulted charts and concluded that a sheltered spot just west of Santa Rosa Island would make for a pleasant night. That evening our friends dinghied over for drinks and conversation. They were proving to be the kind of friends that are charming, generous, and easy to be with. As an added bonus our boats traveled at a similar speed (slow!) so cruising in consort would be natural.

We left the next morning in high winds. When the waterway opened up into the wide expanse of Florida's Choctawhatchee Bay, it became uncomfortably rough. The wiper ran constantly as spray crashed over the bow and onto the windshield. Soon there was so much salt buildup that visibility was impaired, and I had to go out on deck to spray fresh water on the glass. The weather prediction was for the winds to increase through the day, so we decided to duck into Destin Harbor. This harbor is well-protected and has good anchoring but after several nights at tranquil remote spots, the "Disneyland" look and vibe of Destin was kind of shocking. We phoned several waterfront restaurants to enquire about where we might land our dinghy, but no one could tell us. There were signs on the shore warning that no unauthorized landing or docking was permitted.

Carefully studying the shoreline, we discovered a small patch of sand next to a pier extending from a restaurant deck. If we landed our dinghy there, we could sneak through the private property of an adjacent resort and reach the street. From there we would have access to all the stores, bars, and restaurants of Destin. Of course the whole area was festooned with "No Trespassing" signs, but we would just have to ignore them. Jill and I launched the dinghy and stealthily approached our target. Turning off the engine we glided onto the small beach and hidden from view by the piers of the deck, we pulled the dinghy ashore and tied off to a decaying wooden seawall. Then acting as though we were guests at the resort with every right to be there, we walked to the street side of the building, entered the restaurant, and requested a table for two. Our efforts were rewarded with a mediocre meal, indifferently prepared and very expensive. Sadly, that was to be the case more often than not. In the year we traveled there were some memorable meals but most of the lavish waterfront establishments over-promised and under-delivered. A better bet was to find small unpretentious establishments that may not have the ocean view, but whose emphasis was on quality food. Of course, eating on the boat was never disappointing. The views were outstanding, and the dress code was always casual.

The wind died down the following day, and we left the touristy environs of Destin for the laid back homeyness of the Blue Water Bay Marina in Niceville, Florida. The permanent residents of the marina were putting on an elaborate Thanksgiving feast and made a point of inviting all the loopers and other transients to join them. It was wonderful! There were turkeys, oven roasted, deep fried, and grilled, plus cherry, apple, and pumpkin pies, mashed potatoes, stuffing, yams, and cranberry sauce. Jill and I did miss the company of our children, but this had to be one of the nicest holidays on record. We felt a special bond with our looper friends with whom we were sharing the trials and tribulations of this adventure and our local hosts who showed us such genuine warmth and hospitality.

We prepare to drop anchor off a hurricane blasted island in the Florida Panhandle.

We were making our way east towards the big bend of Florida where the east/west orientation of the panhandle turns southward. We anchored in Burnt Mill Creek and Farmdale Bayou before arriving at the Water Street Marina in Apalachicola. I don't recall much about the town except the marina was stupidly expensive and our restaurant meal was another disappointment. Let me clarify: the food was disappointing, but the time spent in the company of friends was always worth the effort. The next day we ran up the coast to Carrabelle, our jumping-off point for the Gulf crossing. The number one task on our agenda was to top up our diesel tanks, fill up water tanks, pump out the holding tank, and get gasoline for the outboard and the Honda generator. That accomplished, we settled down to pick a weather window for a Gulf crossing.

All the weather models predicted smooth weather on the Gulf for our first big open water crossing of the trip. There are two routes across the Gulf that are popular with loopers. The first is a direct route from Carrabelle to Tarpon Springs. This is about 170 miles and can be accomplished in daylight if you have a very fast boat. Slower boats can start in the afternoon, cruise through the night, and arrive at the approaches to Tarpon Springs in late morning. The late morning arrival is recommended because motoring through a minefield of crab traps in the blinding rising sun is an adventure to be avoided.

The second route is known as the rim route and is longer but consists of shorter segments all of which can be accomplished in daylight even in a slow boat. Both options have advantages and disadvantages,

We opted for the rim route for several reasons. We have a boat with a slow seven-knot cruising speed. The route allows us to stop at several small and unique coastal towns. The benign weather was predicted to last for almost a week and that gave us plenty of time to enjoy the stops. Our friends on *Sabot* had the same idea and a young couple on a small trawler asked to join our fleet. Our boats traveled at similar speeds and our outlooks on life and adventure meshed. We made a plan to leave the next day and anchor at Dog Island about eight miles from Carrabelle's harbor. Leaving Dog Island before sunrise would give us a head start on the first 70-mile leg of our Gulf Crossing.

The following day we anchored in a peaceful cove on the north end of Dog Island and took dinghies to the beach for a walk, and so that the crew of *Sabot* could exercise their canine shipmate, Peggy. The idea of a campfire on the beach was very appealing and we set about gathering driftwood. Our activity aroused the curiosity of some island residents who politely but firmly told us no fires were permitted on the beach. It seems as though years ago a wind shift caused a beach fire to ignite some brush and sent it racing across the island destroying several homes. We of course complied and had an informative conversation with the locals about life on the island. They mentioned there was a spring-fed pond on the island that had some resident alligators. This was too much for a group of curious northerners to resist so we fired up our dinghies and made our way down the island to the location of the pond. The insanity of going to an alligator-infested pond in small rubber boats was not lost on us but we proceeded in spite of warnings from the more rational parts of our brains. When we arrived, we saw no alligators, to our great disappointment and relief. We got back to our boats at sunset, secured the dinghies, and set the alarms for a predawn departure. The next day as we cruised over a flat calm gulf, we were visited by several large pods of dolphins who entertained us by frolicking in our bow wake. Throughout the day all three crews communicated on the VHF radio, and it was decided that our little flotilla should be called "Peggy's Pack" after the big black lab on *Sabot*.

The crossing took all day and we arrived at our destination late in the afternoon. We spent the night at the Sea Hag Marina in the fishing village of

Steinhatchee, Florida. The next morning, we felt our way out of the harbor in heavy fog and headed south along the coast to Cedar Key. We anchored off an uninhabited island about a mile from the town of Cedar Key. We dinghied in and walked around the town, looking at shops,-- and getting a bite to eat before heading back to explore the uninhabited island that we had anchored near.

We walked the beach and hiked inland discovering an overgrown cemetery. We later discovered that far from being uninhabited, the island had an active and voracious population of no-see-ums. These tiny flying insects are small enough to pass through all but the finest screens and their bites raise red welts. The next morning my legs and arms looked as though I had the measles. Everyone suffered, but I suffered more. I concluded that some people are more allergic to the bites than others and treated myself with several potions, concocted by Jill, which relieved the itching and seemed to repel the little bastards.

Heavy fog greeted us again the next morning. We decided to postpone our departure until it cleared. At noon, still fogged in, we all decided to stay another day. Next morning it was still foggy but manageable and we headed out into a quiet gulf accompanied by many dolphins and moved south to Crystal River. The entrance channel to Crystal River is very long and tortuous with many shallow spots that might be impassable at low tide. The narrow channel eventually opened up into Kings Bay where we dropped the hook in five feet of water. Crystal River is known as a manatee sanctuary and is home to a hundred or more manatees in the winter months where the spring-fed waters provide a perfect environment for these gentle creatures. The crew of *Sweet Day* swam with the manatees, but Jill and I were satisfied looking at them from our dinghy and from the boardwalk that surrounds the springs. The town had several good restaurants and a very cool tearoom.

The morning of our planned departure we were once again socked in with fog and each crew made a decision on the wisdom of leaving in those conditions. *Sabot* and *Sweet Day* decided to go. Jill and I decided to stay put for another day. It was painful to see our friends leave without us but the decision to stay was the right one for us. We said our goodbyes on the radio and promised to try to meet again in the days and weeks ahead.

Voyage Log #8
Friends and Shipmates,

I've spent decades sailing along the coasts of the Great Lakes. The challenges to the sailor there are principally weather-related. The water is deep and mostly obstruction-free, and the entrances to harbors are usually very straightforward. Of course, the big lakes can serve up some nasty weather that could ruin anyone's day, but a prudent captain can avoid that by carefully monitoring the wind and wave reports that are readily available through various apps.

So why did I find cruising the Gulf of Mexico so anxiety producing? Let me count the ways:

1   Shallow water: Florida's Gulf Coast is very shallow for many miles offshore. It is common to be out of sight of land in water you can stand up in. The charts are well-marked with depths, but storms and currents are constantly changing the contours of the bottom so monitoring the depth sounder is advisable. People who are not sailors often think that deep water is terrifying. The black crushing depths of the abyss live large in the imagination. Sailors know that deep water is their friend. Boats have evolved over the centuries to travel on the surface of the seas. Running aground in shallow water can be a minor irritant or can cascade into a life-threatening situation. A grounded ship is helpless if the weather turns bad before it is afloat. Most Florida Gulf Coast communities have dredged, well-marked channels extending many miles out into the Gulf. These provide enough depth to allow boats of moderate draft to come and go, but unusually low tides can even make the channels untenable.

2   Fog: Every damn morning of our journey along the coast was blanketed with heavy fog. We are 21st-century mariners, and the Alvin James is equipped with radar, AIS, a GPS chart plotter, as well as all the bells and whistles needed to travel in low visibility conditions. This is not a cliche; bells, whistles, and horns are all approved signaling devices the Coast Guard requires you to have. Of course, there is fog on the Great Lakes but maneuvering the torturous narrow channels of the Gulf knowing that wandering a few feet outside could mean running aground adds another layer of stress.

3   Crab pot floats: Shellfish are an important part of Florida's economy. Large swatches of the Gulf are home to tens of thousands of crab and lobster traps. Each trap sits on the bottom and is marked by a float on the surface connected by a line. These must be avoided. Not spotting a float and running over it often results in the line wrapping around your prop and bringing your engine to a stuttering, crashing halt. The only solutions are to dive under your boat with a mask and knife and attempt to cut the tangle off or call for assistance. Because of this threat, a leisurely run down the coast on autopilot is not recommended. This, of course, is complicated by fog when your visibility is limited, and AIS and radar don't help at all.

We did cruise the Gulf Coast. I did find it somewhat stressful, but the charming old Florida towns were worth the effort. Manatees, dolphins, and countless seabirds were our companions.

Stay healthy, Stay happy, Stay in touch.

Two days later, the morning dawned clearer than the days before. The shorelines were visible, and I estimated we had about 200 yards of visibility. Not perfect but doable. The state of the tide would give us sufficient depth to get through the shallows and we could see and identify the navigation markers before we were right on top of them. It took us about an hour to make our way out of the winding channel and into the Gulf. The Gulf waters are shallow many miles from shore. You can find yourself out of sight of land in water you can stand up in! Add to that the limited visibility due to fog and the ever-present crab trap floats and you have the trifecta of sailor's stress. We spent the day avoiding shoals and steering around traps and finally anchored in the lee of Anclote Key. We had now successfully crossed the Gulf and were about to reenter the Gulf Intracoastal Waterway. The heavy fog returned the next morning, but the deteriorating weather forecast meant that our anchorage would not be tenable for too much longer.

Making use of all our instruments: two chart plotters, radar, and AIS, we worked our way south in the narrow channel and arrived safe and sound at the marina in Clearwater. We spent two days in Clearwater taking the trolley to Tarpon Springs and touring the art museums. The whole town had a bit of a creepy vibe because of the religious cult that owns much of the real estate downtown. The morning we left was notable for the heavy fog and the huge number of birds that invaded the marina and perched on every available roost. It was a Hitchcock-like nightmare come to life. Fascinating but more than a little eerie. We left as soon as the fog began to lift.

About eight miles down the channel, the fog returned with a vengeance and reduced visibility to zero! Since we had to negotiate several bridges that were required to be open to allow us through, we decided to pull off in a wide part of the channel, drop the anchor and wait it out. It wasn't long before the fog lifted, and we resumed motoring southward under clear, sunny skies.

Our friends on *Sabot* had spent two days in St. Petersburg and we arranged to reunite when our tracks crossed under the Sunshine Skyway Bridge on Tampa Bay. Once we sighted each other we continued across the bay to a marina in Bradenton. An unremarkable two days were spent there before leaving to anchor out, a few miles away, near the town of Cortez.

In Cortez we met up with our friend and local resident Susan Curry. Susan is an artist of note and she drove us around in her car and introduced us to some great little eating establishments that are not on the tourist radar. A good time was had by all. When we finished our loop Susan sent us a beautiful mosaic she

Mosaic by Susan Curry

created based on a photo of Jill and I and our boat. We were awestruck by her thoughtfulness and her virtuosity. It is one of our most treasured possessions.

    We had lately been having problems with our autopilot. In fact, it initially refused to turn on when leaving Crystal River and once we did get it to work it refused to turn off and wouldn't allow us to return to manual mode. (A stress-inducing situation when trying to avoid crab floats!) I finally disconnected the thing and hadn't used it since. In the evenings I would pore over the instruction manuals hoping to discover some simple fix. No luck. Now perhaps you are wondering why a pleasure boater would require an autopilot? It is a sublime pleasure steering a boat over the waves of open water and gliding gently alongside a dock (presuming you don't hit it!). On long passages on featureless seas however, hand steering becomes a tedious exercise where one's attention must be focused on the compass needle or on the chart plotter screen. I had sailed boats for decades without autopilots, but once acquiring one I have considered it essential to the enjoyment of voyaging.

My current problem was compounded by the fact that the autopilot on *Alvin James* was the original equipment on the boat thus making it 35 years old, a virtual Methuselah in the world of electronics. The model had been out of production for many years and was no longer supported by the manufacturer. A new unit would cost thousands of dollars that I was unwilling to spend. One of the advantages of being a 21st-century mariner is the availability of the Internet and the great nautical garage sale called eBay. It didn't take long to discover a gently used replacement control head for my unit. I also called and made arrangements at a repair facility in Stuart, Florida to do the installation and to attend to several other niggling problems that fell outside my limited expertise.

FedEx would ship the auto pilot to Stuart, and we had an appointment to get the work done on January 4th.

Leaving Cortez, we traveled with *Sabot* for several more days and anchored in Cayo Costa State Park. This lovely wilderness island has a well-protected harbor and miles of sandy beaches. Some friends we met years ago on Lake Michigan, after we had both survived a fierce storm, contacted us. They were nearby on their boat, *Terrapin*, and offered to sail over to Cayo Costa and drop the hook so we could visit. The next day they arrived and anchored just outside the entrance. They felt their sailboat's deep keel would make getting into the harbor a bit sketchy. We got in our dinghy and visited them. It was a grand reunion. They are wonderful, generous people who had spent much time and much of a limited budget prepping their old double-ender sailboat for sailing adventures to the Bahamas and beyond. Less than a year later their beloved *Terrapin* was destroyed when Hurricane Ian ripped through Florida's Gulf Coast. Our friends are fine but the lengthy process of preparing a boat will have to start over.

Voyage log #9
Friends and shipmates,

In order to travel the Great Loop you must go around the state of Florida. Proceeding down the gulf coast you are presented with a choice: continue south to the Keys and then travel north past Miami and Ft. Lauderdale or use the Okeechobee Waterway to cut across the state from Ft. Meyers to Stuart on the Atlantic coast. Jill and I chose the second option.

We had lived for years in the Keys and were looking for a new experience. Also, I have a dread of the Miami/ Ft. Lauderdale waterfronts. I have had many conversations with fellow travelers concerning the boat culture of Florida. Is there a higher percentage of brainless entitled jerks traveling Florida waters or is the percentage of jerks the same as anywhere, but the sheer volume of boaters means there are thousands more clueless idiots blasting around? Hard to say but I feel there is a culture that reinforces boorish behavior. This is a problem all over the state, but Miami/Ft. Lauderdale is the epicenter. We decided we could avoid all that by taking the Okeechobee route.

Lake Okeechobee is the second biggest lake entirely within the borders of the United States. The biggest is our beloved Lake Michigan. There are five locks on the waterway and one just off the waterway that we needed to traverse in order to spend a few days on the shore of the big lake at Clewiston. This route is 'old' Florida, small towns lots of wildlife, and no high-rise condos. We saw many different kinds of birds, many manatees, and Iguanas, but sadly no gators. Locals told us they spend a lot of time hiding in the mud this time of year. Oh well.

New Year's Day finds us in Ft. Pierce on the Atlantic coast. Sunny days, warm weather. Have scheduled some time in a boatyard to do maintenance on Alvin James. Other than that, we're just chillin' before it's time to start the long trek north. Hope all is well with you.

Stay healthy, stay happy, stay in touch.

After two days the no-see-ums became too much for me and we decided to continue on our way. The crew of *Sabot* had plans to spend time in the Florida Keys. Jill and I had lived in the Keys for eight years and felt a different route was called for. We decided to cross the state via the Okeechobee Canal. We had never seen Lake Okeechobee, and the canal emptied into the Atlantic Ocean at Stuart, Florida, where we had a date to repair our boat. Two days after leaving Cayo Costa, we parted ways with *Sabot* and headed to Fort Myers and the entrance to the Okeechobee Canal. We stayed at the upscale Legacy Marina waiting out some bad weather and enjoying Fort Meyers. The marina was another victim of Hurricane Ian, receiving a direct hit on September 28, 2022.

It took five days to cross Florida via Lake Okeechobee and the canal. We spent Christmas in the Roland Martin Marina in Clewiston on the southwestern shore of the lake. Afterward we skirted the eastern shore of the lake to the Port Mayaca Lock and back onto the Okeechobee Waterway. We stopped for fuel in Indiantown where we were approached by a woman who recognized our boat. It seemed that she had cruised to the Bahamas in the company of this boat and the original owner. She even showed us a photo of both their boats anchored in a tranquil island harbor. Small world, this boating community! Within two days we anchored in Pendarvis Cove just outside of Stuart. We had crossed the Gulf and crossed the state and were now only a few miles from the Atlantic Ocean and the start of our travels north.

Our stay at the repair facility lasted several days while technicians replaced the autopilot controls, tracked down a leak in the freshwater system and replaced a washdown pump. Jill and I decided to stay at a nearby Air B&B and rent a car to explore the city. We found a wonderful Asian restaurant in the historic old part of town and were able to have some interesting walks along the water. When the work was complete we settled the bill (not too bad) and continued our journey north on the Intracoastal Waterway.

Our next stop of note was Vero Beach. The marina has a mooring field that is so well-protected that when high winds send huge surf crashing onto the beaches there is hardly a ripple in the harbor. We were assigned to share a mooring ball with a large catamaran and gently rafted up alongside. The cat's crew was welcoming and helpful. They mentioned they were about to leave the boat and travel home for a week. Perfect! I had been concerned that if I needed to run the generator it would not be pleasant for the crew of a boat we were rafted right next to.

Vero Beach is a popular stop for cruising sailors for several reasons. The moorings are inexpensive. The harbor is clean and calm. The town of Vero Beach has an extensive and safe public transportation system...and it's free! The bus stops right by the dinghy dock, and we use it every day for shopping and entertainment. Many cruisers on their way south to the Keys or the Bahamas find Vero Beach so accommodating that they stay much longer than they had planned. Some never get any farther and spend the winter here. It has such a reputation of being hard to leave, it is widely known among cruisers as "Velcro Beach," a fact that everyone felt compelled to tell us.

Voyage Log #10
Friends and Shipmates,

The crew of the Alvin James has spent the last week or so in Vero Beach, Florida. We are rafted up to another boat in the municipal mooring field. Before we arrived, I had never heard of boats rafted up on a mooring. For members of the audience who are unfamiliar with the language of cruising, rafting is tying up alongside another boat. This is normally done at anchor and both boats will swing on the anchor lowered by one of the boats. It is a cooperative venture usually planned in advance by crews that are traveling together. In a mooring field, things are a little different. Upon arrival you contact the marina and request a mooring. Assuming there is room, the marina will assign a mooring ball to you. The catch is that when you locate your assigned mooring, there may be another boat on it or maybe two! The crews of the boats on the mooring only become aware that you will tie up to them when you get their attention and make them aware of your intentions. Then the careful negotiations and the delicate ballet begins. What side would they prefer you to tie up to? Fenders must be placed to prevent damage to the boats. Once maneuvering close enough, lines must be passed and adjusted to minimize fore and aft movement. Once this is accomplished, the crews introduce each other and exchange relevant information like when might you be leaving. If one boat leaves a day earlier the routine of uncoupling must take place.

At that point common sense and general courtesy should prevail. Don't run your loud generator too late or too early. Music and conversation are indulged in with the knowledge that your neighbors are only a few feet away. For civilized people, this should be second nature.

Being on a mooring ball and not in a slip means that forays to the shore are done using the ship's dinghy. The marina has a dock specifically for dinghies and it is a cruisers' crossroads. The dock is usually busy with crews shuttling from their boats to land performing all the sundry chores life requires: taking out the trash, laundry, grocery shopping, trips to the hardware store, looking for a meal at a restaurant, or taking the dog ashore for a little exercise. The endless parade is always entertaining.

Vero Beach is a very accommodating city for a cruiser because it has a free public transportation system that is clean, safe, and efficient, and can get you almost anywhere you want to go. We are enjoying our stay here but at some time we will want to meander north and explore the cities of Melbourne, Titusville, and St. Augustine. But we are in no hurry.

Stay safe, stay healthy, stay happy.

But leave we did and continued north on what is known as Florida's Space Coast. The coast lived up to its name and we saw multiple rocket launches from the Kennedy Space Center. After stops in Melbourne and Titusville, we spent five days in Daytona Beach. Before we arrived, my impression of Daytona Beach was a spring break destination filled with rowdy kids, wet T-shirt contests, and alcohol-fueled bad behavior. I'm sure you can still find that if you're looking for it, but we spent our time in the historic downtown that was experiencing a renaissance of sorts. There were several great restaurants that were worth the price and a really cool art house movie theater that showed some great films that would never get booked at your local multiplex. So, as film aficionados we give Daytona Beach two enthusiastic thumbs up!

Excerpts From Jill's Sketch Journal:

11/16 Fair Hope, Alabama. We scheduled our Covid booster shots, and planned to stay put a couple of days in case we had reactions. Enjoyed exploring Fair Hope, a single taxpayer colony which was a social experiment in the 1920's; joint ownership and common properties. Lots of artists and free thinkers. An epic thing happened: We met the crew of Sabot when Melanie introduced herself and invited us to grocery shop in their rental vehicle. So appreciated! Melanie, Justin,

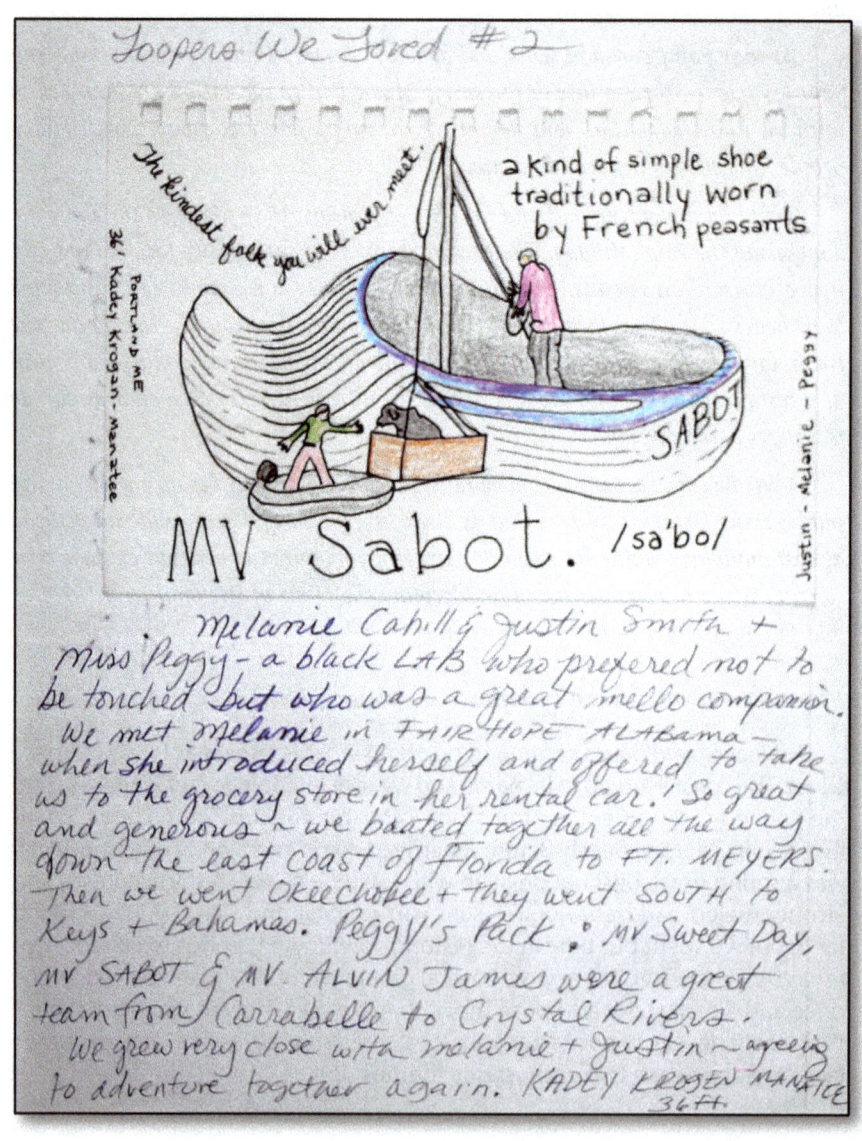

Loopers: Lisa, Annie, Jill, and Melanie shopping before the Gulf crossing.

and their black labrador Peggy were to become great friends. We told them of our scheduled booster shots, and they made appointments too. The next day we walked to a drug store and got Covid boosters together.

Our shared level of boating experience, life experiences, and outlooks quickly became obvious. M/V Sabot is a 36-foot Kadey Krogen Manatee, a great cruising boat with an unusual shape that looks a little like a wooden shoe. Sabot is the word for a simple carved shoe which was made from a single block of wood. The boat had a steering station on the flybridge which had steep steps that Peggy couldn't climb. Justin and Melanie developed an ingenious system to get Peggy up to the steering station using a crane and a plastic box. Back in their Maine home they trained Peggy to get into the box by painting the inside with yummy peanut butter. She loved her elevator rides in the peanut butter box, and we never tired of watching the co-captains lifting Peggy up and down. I made a sketch journal drawing of Sabot doing just that. This would be the second in a series of journal drawings of "loopers we loved."

11/24 As Alvin James & Sabot left an anchorage in Destin Harbor two dolphins jumped from the water and tail-walked next to our boats! We spent Thanksgiving at the Bluewater Bay Marina, a gorgeous little marina near Niceville, Florida where we were invited to join in at a big Thanksgiving dinner celebration with local boaters and visiting loopers. Chased my homesick blues away. Patty, the AGLCA harbor host was extremely generous, taking us into town for laundry and shopping and hosting a social on her boat with other loopers and Eddy, of Eddy's Weather Wag fame.

11/30 The slip at Carrabelle was tricky to get into, with stubby docks and pilings to squeeze between, but with help from caring boaters we were fine. We found lots of loopers here as all were waiting for a safe weather window to cross the Gulf of Mexico. A super fun night at the Fishermen's Wives restaurant with a whole bunch of excited loopers. I think everyone is pumped up for the Gulf crossing. At a captains meeting happy hour we somehow put together a group of three compatible boats and crews to cross with. A quick provisioning trip to the IGA with Lisa, Melanie, and Annie was a hoot – what a great group of adventurous women! It occurs to me that people who choose to do the loop are the kind of courageous people that we have a lot in common with.

12/1 It was decided that we would anchor out at Dog Island with the crews of Sabot and Sweet Day and enjoy the beach and each other before leaving at the crack of dawn to cross the Gulf. This would also shorten the passage. We went on a four-dinghy adventure ride to explore the island, and Peggy's pack was formed. Peggy is a very special Black Labrador who is an almost human member of the crew of M/V Sabot. She led us around various towns, finding dog friendly coffee shops and restaurants, and hanging out as the leader of the pack. Pure fun and folly in this anchorage, though no gators were seen. Sabot, Sweet Day, and Alvin James had a fun, safe, and memorable several days together-one of the very best parts of our Great Loop. Perfect flotilla and a beautiful crossing.

12/5 Gulf crossing to Crystal River, Florida. Lots of dolphins on the Gulf almost every day. I will always remember the day Justin (M/V Sabot co-captain) called me on the VHS as he saw a large group of dolphins headed for our boat. He was on his flybridge and had a bird's eye view. I stood on the bow as 25 dol-

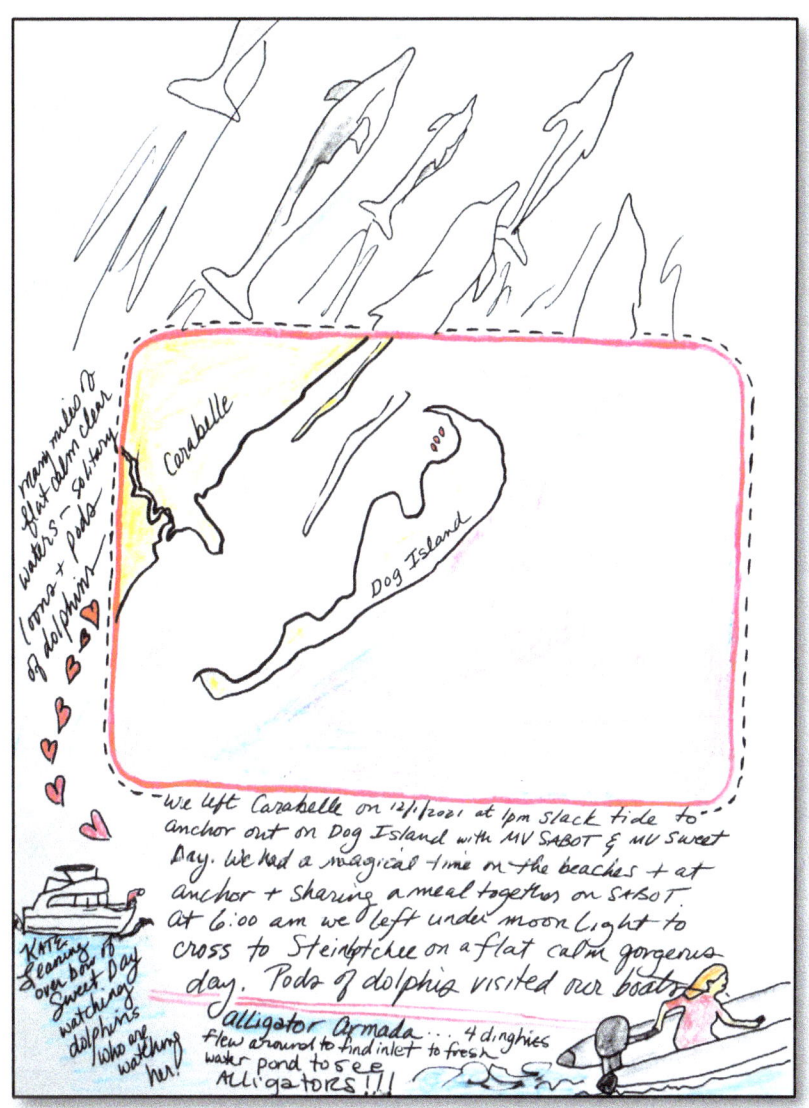

phins rode the bow wake for several magical minutes. Crystal River was a time of seeing manatees and birds and exploring the community with Peggy's Pack.

12/7 The rest of the Pack left in the fog, but we decided to stay and wait for better conditions. It was so sad to see them go, but our safety-first policy meant saying "See you later" to a terrific tribe. We live by the axiom "the most dangerous thing you can have on a boat is a schedule." We learned later that Sweet Day ran over a crab pot float in the dense fog and had to dive under the boat to cut it from the propeller.

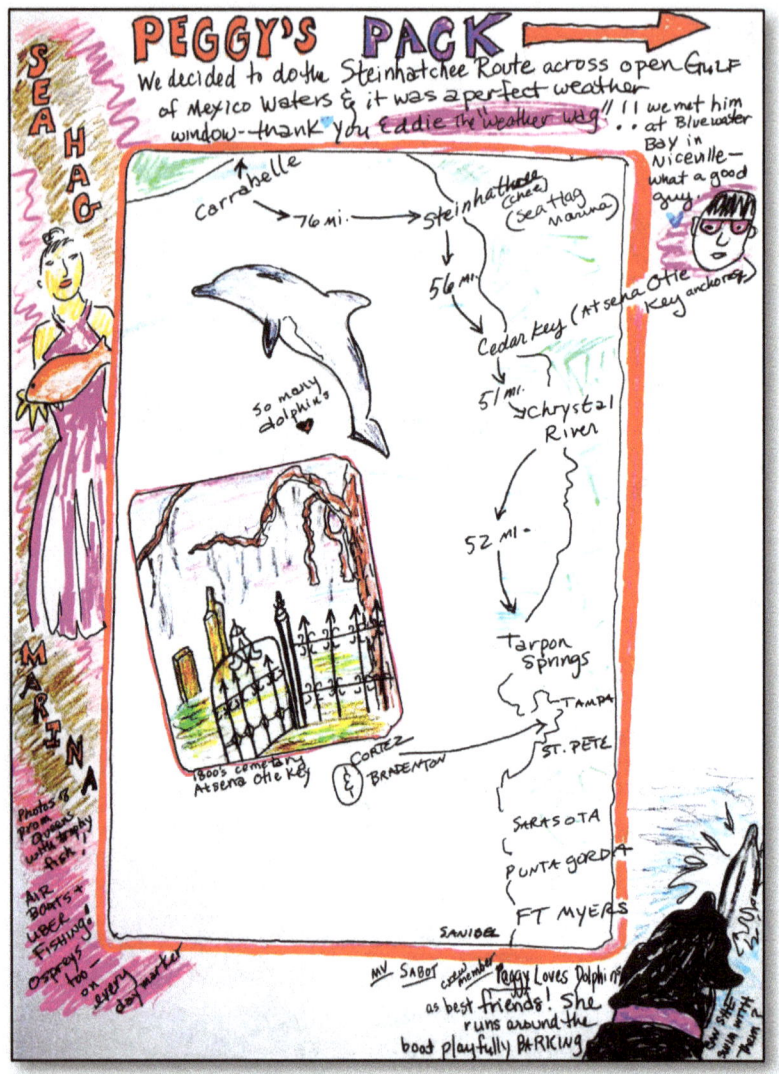

    12/8 Counting the days until the St. Lucie Lock closes for maintenance, and we seem to be in good shape. First no-see-um attacks! Driving us nuts! Walked to Walgreens to gather supplies to make a natural remedy I read about online: ¾ witch hazel, ¼ Listerine, 10 drops of each essential oils: Eucalyptus, Tea Tree, and Lemon Grass. Put in a small mister bottle. As long as we sprayed this on often, they left us alone.

    12/14 Reconnecting with Sabot on Tampa Bay we explored Cortez, Sarasota, and Fort Meyers together. It's great to spend time with Melanie and Justin,

but we all have different priorities and make our own plans as things come up. We happily reconnected with Sabot under the Sunshine Skyway Bridge, and together we enjoyed meeting with my fellow mosaic artist, Susan Curry. I got to know Susan in online Mosaic groups after admiring her work. One of the things I told James was non-negotiable was making time to finally meet Susan Curry in Cortez, Florida. A special day with Susan in a very charming and historic fishing village. Susan is a very prolific and talented artist. Her yard and home were filled with amazing art and she was a great host and companion. Meeting her in person was even better than I had imagined. We would part company again as

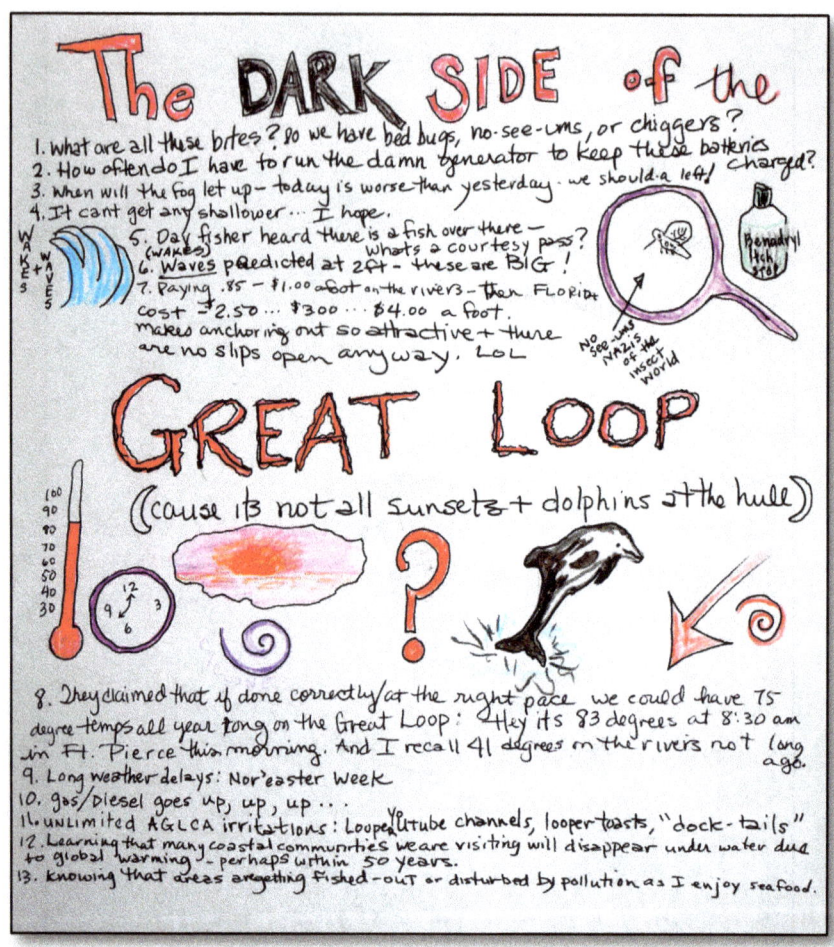

Sabot would head south to the Florida Keys, and we would prepare to cross the state by way of Lake Okeechobee. We planned to meet again eventually on the other side of the state.

12/18 We reconnected with boating friends Julie & Tony, who we met years ago in Green Bay, Wisconsin - dinghied out from our anchorage in Cayo-Costa to chat on the deck of their beautiful sailing vessel, Terrapin. We could not have known that they would survive a hit by a tornado a few days later only to have their boat destroyed later by Hurricane Ian.

12/20–12/26 Often the places we remember are not the ones found on maps- it's the nameless little coves we stumble upon – the ones we discover for ourselves.

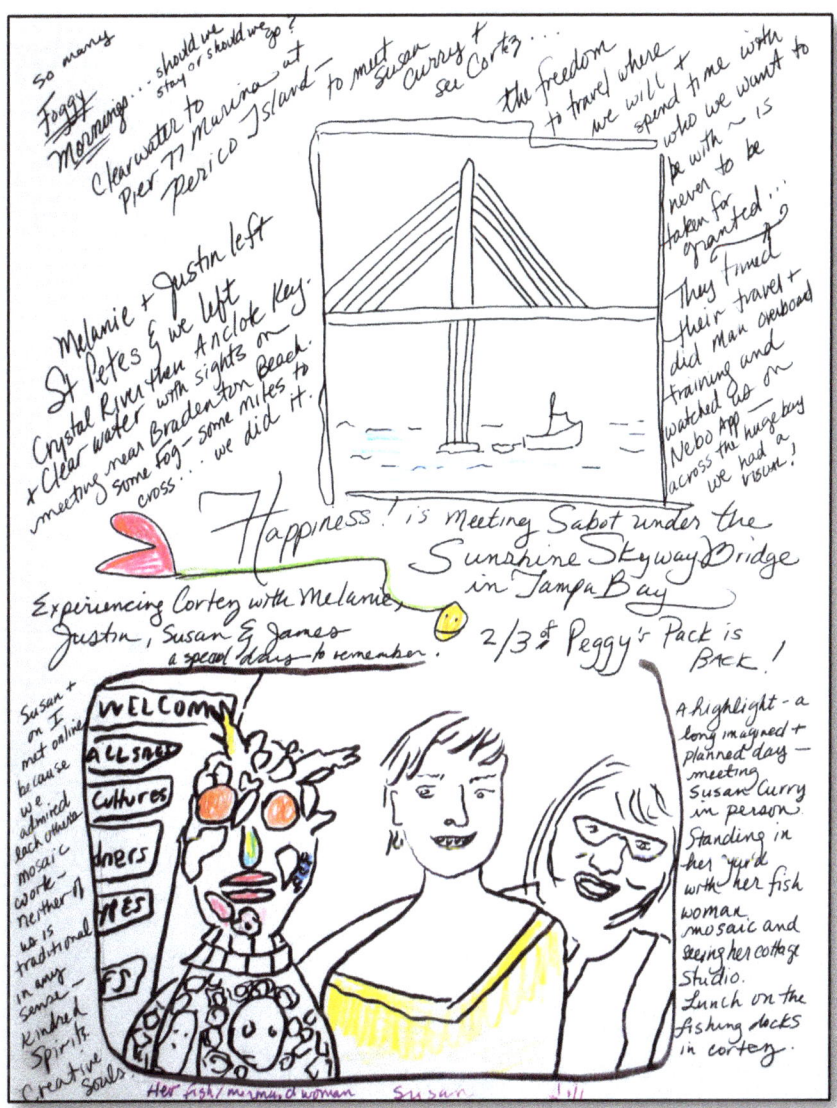

Our time in the Everglades and on Okeechobee was unique and very special. I made a silly Christmas card with my imaginary boat parade to send to a few people electronically. When we lived in the Florida Keys, we always enjoyed holiday boat parades, so I imagined a wild version.

12/24 We were alone in an almost deserted little marina in Clewiston, along the shore of Lake Okeechobee. We soon realized our boat was surrounded by wildlife. Manatees, a bright orange iguana in a tree with his green mate, herons, cranes, coots, cormorants, anhinghas, egrets, vultures, doves, moorhens, and

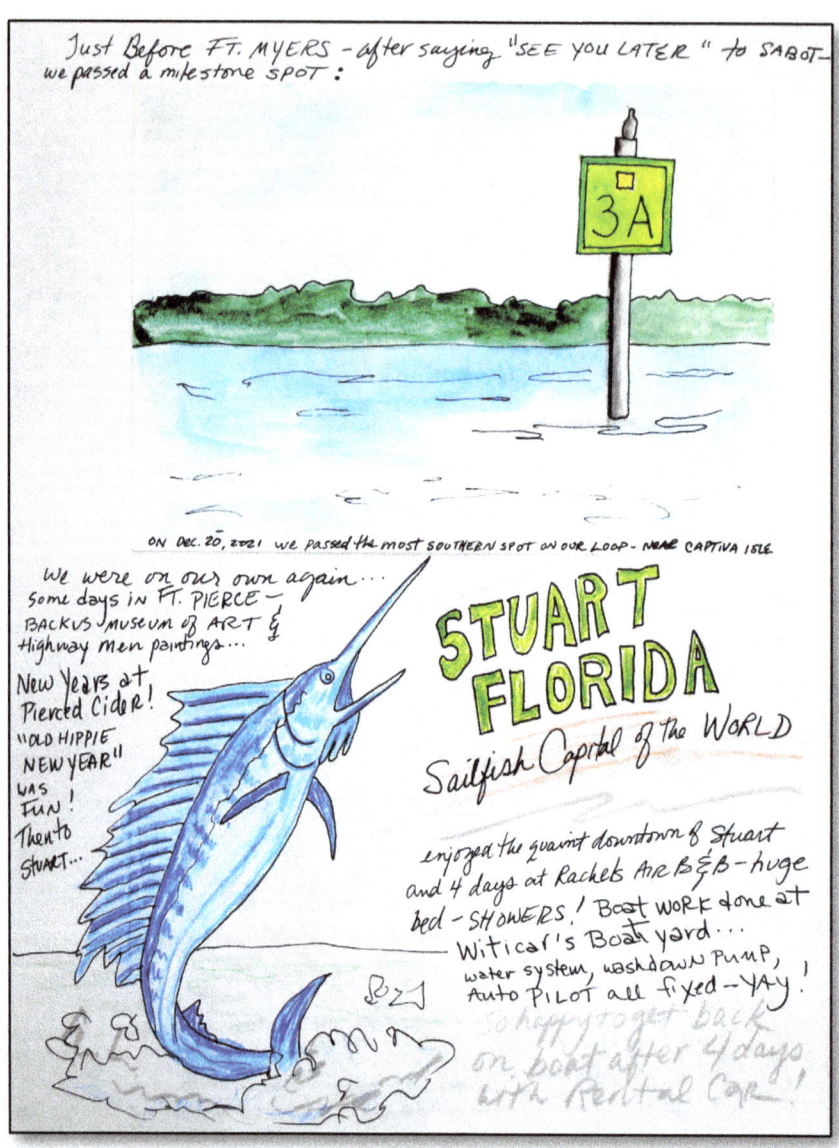

gulls. I will never forget the very entertaining and rascally grackle who had an open packet of Hellmann's mayo that he teased other grackles with for two days! He would put his beak inside and boastfully have a taste and then hop away causing much envy in the bird world, like a child with a new toy that was too good to share.

12/26 We decided to take the rim route on the Okeechobee. Lots of birds in the first section. The Torry Island manually operated swing bridge was amazing

to see. Built in the 1920s. We called the bridge tender's home, and he came down to open it manually. This was just the first of many historic and unusual bridges and locks we would experience on the rest of our loop.

12/30. Our 40th wedding anniversary. Christmas, New Years... we had plenty of time to celebrate and feel grateful and although we missed family and friends, the Great Loop year cemented the most important relationship of my life.. my shipmate for life: James.

Lyrics from a Christy Moore song which was emailed to us by a friend in New Jersey:

I am a sailor, you're my first mate.
We signed on together, we coupled our fate.
Hauled up our anchor, determined not to fail.
For the heart's treasure together we set sail.
With no maps to guide us we steered our own course.
Ride out the storms when the winds were gale force.
Sat out the doldrums in patience and hope.
Working together we learned how to cope.
Life is an ocean and love is a boat in troubled water that keeps us afloat.
When we started the voyage there was just me and you.
Now gathered around us we have our own crew.
Together we're in this relationship.
We built it with care to last the whole trip.
Our true destinations not marked on the charts.
We're navigating the shores of the heart.

Our anniversary caused me to reflect a bit. It's hard to believe how far we have come, and how quickly the days have passed. Living on a boat without the easy distractions of home forces us to pay attention and live in another way. It offers a unique opportunity to focus on life in the moment with an open mind, to see where it would take me next… A year of intense looking……hours at the helm… I was often excitedly scanning and trying to take it all in. I have a lust for all I see.

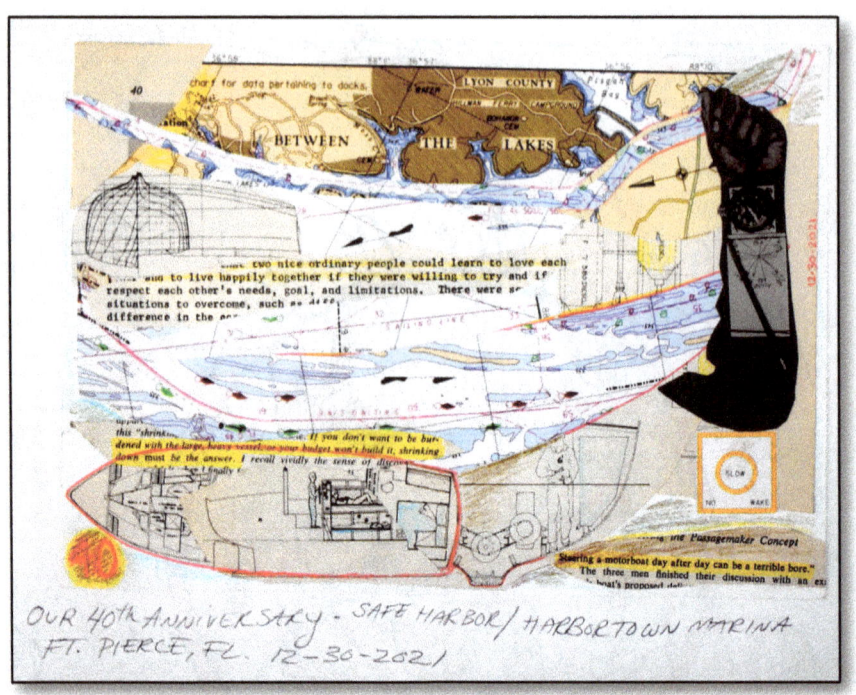

OUR 40th ANNIVERSARY - SAFE HARBOR / HARBORTOWN MARINA
FT. PIERCE, FL 12-30-2021

1/4 Stuart, Florida – Our southernmost point! Had the boat worked on... We spent four days off the boat, staying at an Air B&B with a rental car. Saw black-bellied whistling ducks on the river near our B&B!

1/8 Vero Beach. A week at a mooring ball makes me realize why boaters stay here (Velcro Beach). Free buses, affordable mooring balls, botanical garden, easy days of walking and exploring, and lots of creative time.

1/22–1/24 Space Coast. We saw several rockets take off right from our floating home. I had some days to use some vintage nautical charts that were on the free shelf at the marina club house to make a series of collages with drawn elements. When weather forces us to sit still, it's time to explore and get creative.

1/24 Wow, this was a thumbs up day! Between Titusville and New Smyrna, we saw Roseate Spoonbills overhead, had dolphins riding our bow wake and then I turned around and there was an athletic couple in an outrigger kayak riding on our stern for 35 minutes, paddling while being pulled along by our momentum. What will happen next? On to Daytona...

1/26–1/31 Daytona Beach Halifax Marina is a large, well-maintained place that is an easy walk from an historic neighborhood. The city is spending millions on the river historical district. Very pleasant wide streets with palm trees and brick sidewalks: the esplanade. A fine small art cinema and a great Japanese Ramen Restaurant encouraged us to stay awhile. (A nice surprise since the name Daytona made me think of spring breakers and cars on the beach.)

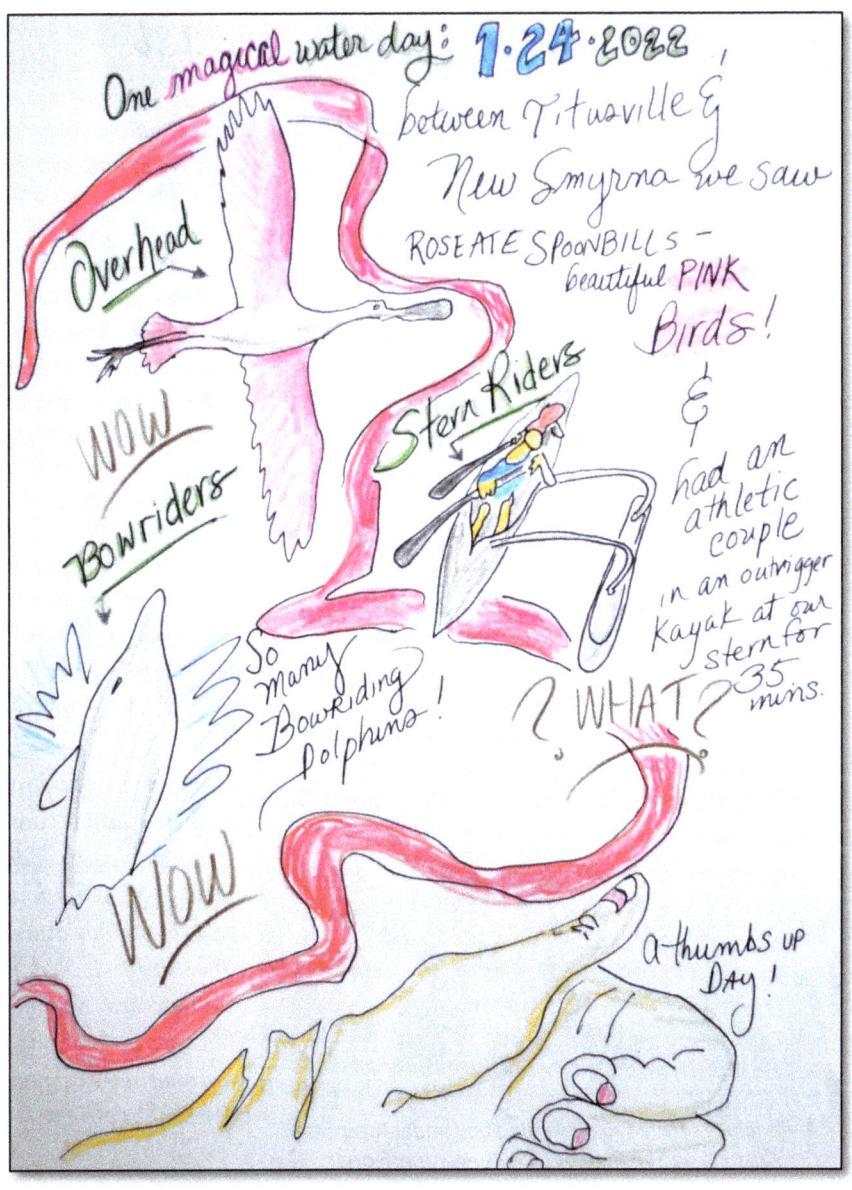

Up the Atlantic Coast

A ship in a harbour is safe but that is not what ships are built for.
John A. Shedd

Voyage log #11
Friends and Shipmates,

As I write this, Alvin James is in the north mooring field of Saint Augustine. It is a thoroughly miserable day. A cold front has slammed into the area with high winds and rain. The boat's motion requires care must be taken when preparing meals and eating to keep food from jumping off the stove or counters. We are careful to conserve electricity because the heavy cloud cover makes solar energy collection pretty anemic.

Alvin James secured to a mooring ball under the guns of Castillio de San Marcos in St. Augustine, Florida

Going ashore is not an option because a dinghy ride would be pretty harrowing and very wet, so, we will spend our day on the boat. We have a diesel heater that keeps us toasty, and plenty of provisions to keep us nourished. The spirit locker is well-stocked and we have many books and a strong Wi-Fi signal. We will be alright.

We left Vero Beach after an enjoyable week and traveled north to Melbourne. Then it was on to Titusville for three days that were not as enjoyable. The marina was right across from the Kennedy Space Center, and we did witness a rocket launch. The marina however was still in recovery from hurricane devastation and was in pretty poor shape.

I was looking forward to spending time in St. Augustine and have not been disappointed. It is a beautiful city with a historic downtown that is great for walking and biking. We are moored just off the Castillo de San Marcos, a 16th-century Spanish fort that protected the harbor for hundreds of years. Next week we will head up to Jacksonville and spend the rest of February exploring the St. John's River before starting the long journey up the Atlantic coast to New York City and on to the Great Lakes.

Stay safe, stay healthy, stay happy.

St. Augustine is the oldest permanent European settlement in North America. It is a charming city with much to see and do. Our mooring ball was about a quarter mile from the dinghy dock and that put us right in the center of the historic part of town. The town is very walkable, and we also rode our bikes. Our favorite transportation was the tourist train which gives a narrated tour of the city and allows you to hop on and off anywhere you wish. On days when the wind and waves would have meant a wet dinghy ride, we took advantage of the marina's free water taxi. A call to the marina office would result in the dispatch of a boat to ferry us from our boat to shore and back to our boat in the evening when our explorations were over. After ten days of history, art, fine food, and beautiful architecture, we needed to start moving once again. Jill had heard that Florida's St. Johns River was a naturalist's delight. It is a rare north-flowing river whose headwaters are near Lake Okeechobee, and which flows into the Atlantic Ocean at Jacksonville, Florida. We broke the trip to Jacksonville into two days, stopping for the first night at the Palm Cove Marina on the city's outskirts. I was unaware until that moment that Jacksonville is the largest city in the contiguous U.S. by area. The result was we spent a day getting to the southern border of the city and another day arriving at the Metropolitan Park Marina near the city center.

The Metropolitan Park Marina was almost deserted with only one other boat when we arrived. Some of the slips were so silted in that they were no longer usable. Recent hurricanes had taken their toll on the infrastructure, but the slips that were available were in good condition and there were no fees! Even the electricity for shore power was available at no cost. There was no marina staff or security on site, but the neighborhood seemed safe, and we experienced no problems during our three-day stay.

The St. Johns River is very wide and lake-like as it winds its way through Jacksonville but narrows considerably about 40 miles south as it approaches the town of Palatka. We stayed at the Boat House Marina in Palatka and prepared the boat for company. Some friends had accepted our invitation for a week-long cruise up the St. Johns River. Ken and Cathy are very dear old friends and shipmates. We had cruised the Caribbean together several times and sailed extensively on Lake Michigan. Ken and I had sailed across the Atlantic Ocean together twice. We were four people who knew how to coexist comfortably and peacefully in a small space. On the day of their arrival, we went shopping and provisioned the boat with food and drink. The following day, as we completed our preparations, some of the resident boaters suggested a happy hour on the dock where they could share local knowledge about what lay ahead. The evening started amicably but ended abruptly when the wooden picnic table we were sitting at collapsed thanks to an undetected rotten crossbeam that gave way. The bench and its occupants fell on Cathy's leg, crushing her foot, and sent us looking for an emergency room. X-rays showed that the bone was shattered and any thoughts of continuing our adventure were rendered mute. Spending the night on the *Alvin James* was out of the question as it takes a bit of athleticism to board and disembark. For some reason I never discovered, every hotel room within a hundred miles was booked. Ken with assistance from his daughter on the phone, located a vacancy in St. Augustine almost 100 miles away, and he and Cathy left. The next day they drove home to North Carolina. We had a tearful farewell but promised we would see each other again when we passed near their home in the coming months. Jill and I wished Cathy a speedy and full recovery and returned to our boat saddened by how things had turned out.

Our next anchorage was in Seven Sisters Creek. The channels that wind between these seven islands created many opportunities to lower the anchor in peaceful water and relax in a beautiful natural setting. Farther down the river were the Renegades on the River Marina, highly recommended by the locals in Palatka. Unfortunately, the place was wallpapered with mean-spirited political signs that implied if you weren't on their team, you weren't a real American and you were not welcome. Had we not already arranged for a slip, we would have left. As it was, we kept to ourselves and left at first light.

Our next stop was Hontoon Island State Park. We turned off the St. Johns at the park and motored down the Dead River. The river gets its unappealing name because it has almost no current. The river is anything but dead. We saw many alligators basking along the shores. Most logs had a resident turtle, and the sky, water, and woods were filled with birds. At nightfall, the sounds of the surrounding jungle grew in intensity. The grunts of gators and the clacking of wood storks prowling the banks surrounded us. But the prize sound was the blood-curdling shriek of a bird called the limpkin. It felt like we were in Jurassic Park! At night we went out on deck with our spotlight and shining it on the water revealed the glowing reflection of alligator eyes gliding silently by our boat.

An alligator rests on a log along the Dead River in Florida's Hontoon Island State Park.

It was the kind of off-the-beaten-path adventure we had hoped to find, and we both agreed to stay another day.

Leaving the state park we continued south to the city of Sanford, Florida. Our covered slip at the marina protected us from the blistering sun and made life aboard the *Alvin James* most comfortable. Sanford is an undiscovered jewel. It has a beautiful waterfront, a very cool downtown with a great German restaurant, a rollicking Irish Bar with live entertainment, a delicatessen, an authentic Greek restaurant, a Jamaican café, a bakery, and opportunities for provisioning and shopping. We also were fortunate enough to arrive in town during the annual "Porch Fest" music festival. In one of the town's lovely historic neighborhoods, porches, and verandas of homes became stages for a wide variety of music. One can stroll down streets, shaded by towering trees, traveling from venue to venue checking out the music and basking in the cool, laid-back vibe. Food trucks offered a wide variety of delectables and drinks. We were awed by the quality of the performances and agreed it was the best music festival we had ever attended.

The marina was frequently visited by alligators, and one evening we were entertained by the exuberant frolicking of manatees. We discovered later what we had witnessed was part of their sexual ritual! A manatee orgy! We enjoyed Sanford so much we stayed for two weeks. We met some other loopers who had arrived two years previously and found Sanford's charms so alluring they decided to rent a permanent slip and make it their home. During our extended stay we were visited by the crew of the motor yacht *S.L.O. Dancer*, who we had befriended earlier in our voyage. They had traveled hundreds of miles out of their way to visit us. How very sweet!

Voyage Log #12
Friends and Shipmates,

The Alvin James is traveling down Florida's St. Johns River. This magnificent river flows northward from just above Lake Okeechobee to where it spills into the ocean at Jacksonville. People like to say to cruise the St. John is to see "old Florida."

If new Florida is walls of high-rise condos along the ocean and ostentatious displays of wealth, then the river takes you to an area that is definitely not that.

Yes, there are stretches that are developed and look like the blandest suburban tract with docks instead of driveways and punctuated every now and then by a huge McMansion with "look at me" architecture. Then there are the waterfront bars that celebrate irresponsible drinking and display a rabid allegiance to a crooked New York real estate developer. But there are also stretches of river that seem untouched by man. Hauntingly beautiful shores filled with a tangle of plant life. We drop anchor in small tributaries that find us all alone. As the sun sets, the sounds of the jungle predominate. All manner of birds call to attract mates or to claim dominance over territory. At night, our spotlight reveals the glittering eyes of an alligator as it moves silently past our boat. At the southern terminus of the river is Lake Monroe, along its shores is the charming city of Sanford. Filled with art and wonderful restaurants, the city hosts festivals all year round. It is a place that beckons you to linger longer than you planned. Jill and I will spend several weeks here. Oh, did I mention there is a great Irish pub with live music? It doesn't get much better than that.

Stay well, stay safe, be happy.

We did leave, and retraced our steps down the river. On our third travel day as we approached Jacksonville, I discovered an alarming leak and started the pumps. We were in no danger of sinking but we would need to address the issue. We got a slip at the Ortega Landing Marina just outside of Jacksonville and I investigated the leak. It seemed there were two problems: one easy, and one more difficult. The easy problem was a needed adjustment to the shaft seal. The difficult one was a crack in the stern tube that was allowing water into the bilge. The adjustment of the shaft seal could be accomplished in the slip but replacing or repairing the stern tube required pulling the boat out of the water. A day of phone calls revealed that all the boatyards within a hundred miles were booked for several months and would not be able to haul us until late summer or fall. This looked as though it might be the end of our adventure. The marina we were staying at was very nice but also very expensive, and staying there for months waiting until a boatyard could take us was a very unwelcome prospect. A fellow looper who we had met on the Mississippi happened to be in the marina and stopped over to talk. After hearing my tale of woe, he mentioned that he had a friend who had some property on the St. Johns River that had several docks with electricity, and he might be willing to let us keep the boat there for a modest fee until we could arrange for a haul out. He said his friend also knew his way around boats and was a creative problem solver who might be willing to look at my boat. His description of his friend began to sound eerily familiar. The sailor, woodworker, pilot, and former resident of Indiana seemed to match the description of my long-lost cousin whom I hadn't seen or heard from in forty years. A phone call confirmed that indeed was the case and arrangements were made for a visit the next day. After inspecting the problem my cousin felt a fix could be accomplished without pulling the boat by creating a patch to cover the leak. His suggestion made sense to me and Jill, and I spent the evening in the company of my cousin and his wife and our looper friends agreeing that this was a magical and wholly unexpected part of our trip. We also vowed not to let another forty years elapse before we saw each other again. The next day I gathered materials and, with the help of a marine mechanic, fixed the leak. Before we departed, we got a message from some friends from our hometown who were traveling in their camper through Florida and would like to get together. We arranged for an additional day at the marina and had a great time hanging out and catching up.

Voyage Log #13
Friends and Shipmates,

Any long voyage has elements of challenge and of serendipity. In the last week we experienced both.

The Challenge:

We spent several idyllic weeks in the town of Sanford near the source of the St. Johns River. As appealing as the town was, we needed to start our long northern voyage up the Atlantic coast and go back home. It took four days to reach Ortega Landing Marina in Jacksonville, where we planned to spend a few days of R&R and provision the boat. About 50 miles from Jacksonville, I lifted the floorboards to do a cursory examination of the bilge. I discovered that the shaft seal (a piece of equipment that keeps water from entering the boat from where the propeller shaft exits the hull) was spraying a worrying amount of water. I started the pumps and was relieved to discover that the level of water in the bilge started to go down. We were not sinking. The shaft seal was new, and I had no experience with it. Previous boats used a "stuffing box" to achieve the same goal. I could adjust a stuffing box but was unfamiliar with the nuances of the leaking shaft seal. I called ahead to locate a marine mechanic that might help me. The day after we arrived in Ortega Landing, a mechanic met us, and we looked at the problem. The shaft seal did need adjustment and the procedure was something I can do myself in the future. However, I discovered to my horror, that there was another leak in the stern tube. This is a major issue that would require the boat to be hauled out of the water and the propeller shaft pulled and the stern tube replaced. This is not only a pricey proposition, but would require a major interruption of our trip. Every boatyard I contacted had a waiting list of several months to haul a boat. Not only that, but there was no reasonable place to store the boat until such a time. A depressing situation.

Serendipity: boat, Tricia Anne, happened to be in the same marina and the captain, Tim, stopped by to see if he might help. He said he had a good friend who had a home and studio on the St. Johns River. His friend had several docks with electricity, and we might convince him to allow us to keep the boat there until we could schedule a haul out to repair the stern tube. He explained his friend was a really good guy who was a pilot, a sailor, and a master woodworker. In fact, his friend's name was Michael Anthony, and he was coming to the marina the very next day for a visit. As Tim continued to talk about his friend it dawned on me that Michael Anthony might be my long-lost cousin who I had not seen in over forty years! A phone call confirmed this was the case and we would meet up the following day.

The next day after hugs, beers, and an exchange of stories he looked at my boat and came up with some solutions that would not require a time-consuming and expensive haul-out. Within two days, the problem was solved, and we were on our way north to continue our adventure.

Mike and I promised to not let forty years pass before our next reunion. A totally unexpected event in our looping adventure!

Stay healthy, stay safe, stay happy!

We left the marina and continued on the St. Johns River until the turnoff to the ICW just west of the Atlantic Ocean. We anchored for the night in Alligator Creek before arriving the next day at the town of Fernandina Beach, our last stop in Florida. The town was pretty and interesting enough to justify a three-day stay.

In Georgia we anchored for the night at the Plum Orchard estate on Cumberland Island. The entire barrier island is a national park and is home to wild horses and armadillos that can be seen scurrying through the underbrush of the forested island. We visited the Plum Orchard Mansion, once home to the Carnegie family, which can now be toured by park visitors. We were now traveling through a different landscape. The lowlands of Georgia and the Carolinas are composed of barrier islands and rivers that wind their way through miles of salt marsh. This ecosystem protects the mainland from the full fury of the Atlantic Ocean and has a haunting quality that some find boring, but we thought uniquely beautiful. We made a stop at the Brunswick Landing Marina. The town of Brunswick, Georgia is the home of that famous Southern dish: Brunswick Stew. The only restaurant within walking distance required reservations and we had none. So, no stew. The marina is justly famous for offering boaters free beer! The beer was welcome but was not enough of an enticement to keep us around for more than one night. The next day we traveled about 40 miles and anchored in Tea Kettle Creek. We left the ICW and traveled about a quarter mile up the small creek and put the anchor down in what appeared to be the middle of the salt marsh. The tidal range in Georgia is pretty big, from four to eight feet, so we picked our spot carefully to insure we were still afloat at low tide. It was peaceful and surprisingly bug-free.

We arrived at the Sunbury Crab Company Marina the next day and ate at the highly regarded Crab Company restaurant. We shared a table with the crews of several other boats and enjoyed the local seafood. Our next stop was the Coffee Bluff Marina just outside of Savannah. We had wanted to visit Savannah and I thought this little out-of-the-way marina would be convenient. Well, my navigation on the water had so far proved to be good enough to keep us out of trouble but my land navigation was pretty rusty. Downtown Savannah was only a few miles away as the crow flies but as the Uber drives it was a 40-minute trip as the road had to wind around sounds and bayous. Once in town, we traveled on a tour bus and had a very good day topped off with another expensive but disappointing meal. On return to our boat, we discovered that the next two days would consist of high winds and rain. Jill and I decided to hold up and wait for a break in the weather. When the day arrived to leave, we had to contend with the fact that the marina had a very strong current ripping through its tight confines. My tide chart indicated slack tide at 9:00 a.m. At nine the current was still running fast, and it was another 40 minutes before the water was still enough to leave without being swept into anything. The end of the day found us securely anchored behind Buck Island near Hilton Head, South Carolina. We then made our way to Beaufort, South Carolina where we once again rendezvoused with our friends on *Sabot*. Beaufort, South Carolina (pronounced Bewfort. This is important!) is a very cool and pretty town oozing with Southern charm. We took an architectural and history tour and saw the beautiful house where The Big Chill was filmed. We also noticed that this community was belatedly recognizing the contributions of their Black citizens. A refreshing change from the old South I lived in as a child.

The South Carolina coast is beautiful with many pristine anchorages tucked between countless islands and crisscrossed by serpentine rivers and creeks.

The next eleven days were spent making our way north on the ICW through South and North Carolina. The nature of this portion of the waterway is the alternation of narrow, twisting, tidal creeks and large sounds open to the Atlantic. Care must be taken to check weather and tides, as wind against tide can make for a very unpleasant passage through the open water sections. We stopped for a week in Beaufort, North Carolina. (Pronounced Bowfort!) During the Civil War a stranger mispronouncing the name could be accused of being a Northern spy and shot!

Voyage Log #14
Friends and Shipmates,

As I write, the Alvin James is tied up at the town docks in Beaufort, North Carolina. Since I last wrote, we have traversed the coastline of Georgia and South Carolina. Georgia has a tidal range of eight-plus feet and shifting shoals that make life for a Great Lakes sailor difficult. Big tides mean strong currents that often rip through marinas and make docking a white-knuckle adventure. When anchoring, you must be certain that the expected water at low tide will still float your boat.

The coastal towns of Georgia and the Carolinas are beautiful and filled with very friendly people. Some of the barrier islands have herds of wild horses and large populations of birds that thrive on the waters teaming with sea life. Weather-wise we are threading the needle; heading north fast enough to escape the oppressive heat and humidity that are part of summers in the South but not traveling so fast that we run into the remnants of the Northern winter. We are spending a week in Beaufort, North Carolina, to visit with our old sailing buddies, Ken and Cathy. I crossed the Atlantic twice with Ken, and Jill and I have spent months on the Caribbean on their beautiful sailboat, Sojourner. After our visit, we will head up the Carolina coast to Norfolk, Virginia, and the start of the Chesapeake. Now, every mile we travel is a mile closer to friends and family. The epic nature of this trip (a whole year on the boat!) makes the thought of home more appealing than ever.

Stay in touch. Stay healthy and happy.

Beaufort, North Carolina is often referred to as the coolest small town in America. Though that has the sound of a Chamber of Commerce concoction, it is hard to argue with the description. A marina and boardwalk run right along downtown. Restaurants, pubs, ice cream parlors, interesting shops, and a really good maritime museum are all just a short walk from your boat. For excursions farther afield, the marina offers transient boaters the use of a fleet of courtesy cars. There are ferry rides to uninhabited barrier islands where you can see wild horses and explore miles of pristine beaches.

Our friends, Ken and Cathy live on an island nearby and since Cathy's recovery from the disaster in Palatka was going well, they drove over to visit us. *Sabot* was also in port and the six of us had a grand time. *Sabot* left the next day anxious to get home to Maine. Ken and Cathy returned home, Jill and I chose to stay another day. The entire time we were there, the pump out facility was not working. When we finally left the warm embrace of Beaufort, we traveled two miles to another marina to fill our diesel tanks and empty our holding tank. The *Alvin James* had fuel, water, and an empty holding tank and we were rested and ready to continue our adventure.

Next, we snagged a spot on the free dock at Oriental, North Carolina. The town has no Asian roots but was named after the Steamboat Oriental that was wrecked nearby. This has not stopped the municipality from cashing in on the Asian theme with sculptures and paintings of stylized Chinese dragons scattered around town. It is also known as the "Sailing Capital of North Carolina." This claim has a firmer grip on reality. There are more sailboats than people in town and the Neuse River is wide and windy and a wonderful environment for sailing. The free dock in the harbor is a magnet for people strolling along the waterfront and we were visited by many curious locals who enquired about our trip and offered to drive us to grocery stores or any other errands we needed to run. We stayed for two days and concluded it was the friendliest town we had ever visited.

Belhaven was our next stop. We embarked on a walking tour of the town and were stopped by a young Black man in a pickup truck. He gave a friendly greeting and a smile and asked if we were new in town. We said we were. He introduced himself as the mayor and said he hoped we enjoyed our stay and if there was anything he could do for us, we just needed to go to the city hall and he or his staff would do what they could. This kind of radical hospitality costs nothing, makes for a memorable visit, and enhances the reputation of the city as a stop worth making.

A month after leaving Florida, we arrived at the Pongo River and the entrance to the 21-mile-long Alligator-Pongo River Canal. This arrow straight canal leads to the Alligator River which empties into Albemarle Sound. The sound is about 20 miles wide and it is suggested that a mariner pay close attention to weather before crossing. All the weather models we looked at predicted storms in the evening, which gave us a narrow window to get to the other side and find a suitable place to spend the night. We decided to go. This was perhaps the worst decision we made on the whole trip. By relying on the weather forecast most favorable to my agenda, I got sucked into exceeding the boundaries of my own best assessments of acceptable risk. Note to self: Don't do that again!

The first hour after entering the sound it was lumpy and gray and just what the weather apps predicted. Our radar screen showed several small storm cells that crossed our path either in front or behind us. Then a huge disturbance on the radar screen appeared behind us and was tracking in our direction. It became obvious we would not be able to outrun it. The sky grew very dark, and we were pelted with rain. The wind increased and so did the size and steepness of the waves. Soon we were surfing down the faces of great waves and fighting the wheel as we slewed sideways trying to keep the boat in control and not broaching. Adding to the problem were the crab trap floats that were painted black and were all but invisible in the failing light and driving rain. Steering was a physical workout and Jill and I would swap positions every 10 minutes. One of us would steer and the other would point out obstacles to be avoided. Eventually we reached the entrance to the Pasquotank River. The river was wide and didn't offer much shelter from the wind and waves but what little was there was appreciated. About four miles up the river we dropped anchor. The boat bucked but the bow shuttlecocked into the wind and the anchor held. The storm continued for a few hours before it blew itself out and we spent a much-needed quiet night.

When morning arrived, we motored about eight miles to Elizabeth City. The city has a free dock, and the town has enough to hold your interest for a bit but the main reason for stopping is that it is the jumping off point for a transit of the Great Dismal Swamp canal. This canal was constructed in the 1700s and was an important commercial corridor in the early history of the country. Today it is used exclusively by pleasure boats and paddlers. It is narrow and the canopy of trees on the banks sometimes touch overhead creating a tunnel-like effect. It is shallow, seldom deeper than six feet, and it is unwise to follow another boat too closely because the turbulence of the prop wash can cause logs on the bottom to lift up and become a hazard.

We spent the night at the visitors center about halfway through the canal and visited a small nature center on the grounds. We left early the next morning to avoid the closing of the canal to motorized traffic due to an annual kayaking event that draws hundreds of participants. We thought about staying an extra day to watch the spectacle but thought better of it when it looked as though we only had one good travel day before a building nor'easter shut everything down. The canal was as quiet and still as a chapel while we motored along at five knots and reached the Elizabeth River.

Voyage Log #15
Friends and Shipmates,

Today, May 6*th*, we head to Portsmouth, Virginia, via the Dismal Swamp Canal. The canal is narrow, silent, and mysterious. It teems with wildlife, and we motor slowly beneath a canopy of trees growing right to the water's edge. Part of the haunting nature of this place lies in its history. The canal through the swamp was conceived by George Washington who gathered investors to finance this daunting engineering project. It was dug with picks and shovels by enslaved people to profit wealthy investors. Today, Jill and I use signals beamed from satellites to aid our navigation of the area.

In later years, the swamp was a vital link in the Underground Railroad, perhaps giving some of the children and grandchildren of the enslaved canal builders a pathway to freedom.

A screen shot from my phone of a weather app showing the reason we stayed in port for a week.

Several days before our transit of the Dismal Swamp, Jill and I had a harrowing experience on Albemarle Sound. This large body of water has a fearsome reputation and is not to be trifled with. My reading of several weather apps gave me confidence that a late afternoon crossing would be drama-free. Things were going well until a storm cell overtook us with high winds, rain, hail, and five to six-foot waves. The boat was slewing sideways, and it took both of us alternating at the helm to keep us on *course. After crossing the sound, but still battered by waves, we dropped anchor about two miles up the Pasquotank River. Our anchor held us in one spot, but we were bucking like a bronco until late into the night. The storm finally lost its power, and we settled down for a sleep.*

This weekend we will hunker down in Portsmouth, Virginia, for a week waiting for a powerful Nor'easter to blow itself out. Such are the trials and tribulations of cruising.

Be safe, healthy, and happy.

The Norfolk/Portsmouth area in Virginia is home to the largest U.S. Navy yard in the world. As the wind began to build, we cruised past huge gray warships being refitted. Small patrol boats fitted with machine guns patrolled along the shore ensuring no boats on the river approached too close. I had made reservations at the Ocean Yacht Marina in Portsmouth. When we arrived, the wind was howling but we managed to get the boat into the slip and tied up without embarrassing ourselves. In 2014, I had stayed at this same marina for a week while three friends and I prepped our boat for a transatlantic sail to Portugal. It was comforting to see that the bathrooms were just as filthy and in the same state of disrepair as they had been when I was here last. Who says you can't go home again?

Unsanitary facilities aside, the Portsmouth and Norfolk area was a great stop. A raging storm on the Atlantic Coast kept us in harbor for a week, but these towns have so much to offer a visitor it wasn't a burden at all. Norfolk is just across the river from Portsmouth and is accessible by a ferry boat that runs every fifteen minutes. The Chrysler Art Museum is a jewel with a world-class collection. A tour of the battleship Wisconsin is amazing if for nothing else just the scale of the ship! It is huge! We took a boat tour of the navy yard. We went to a movie theater in Portsmouth and ate and drank our way around both cities. The night before we left, the Atlantic Union Pavilion, a concert venue right behind our marina, featured the band Chicago. Though I was never a fan of their music, the band was in fine form and sounded great. We were able to sit in comfort on our aft deck and hear the music as though we had seats at the pavilion.

We left Portsmouth in a light fog that confounded my prediction that it would soon burn off. In fact, it grew steadily more opaque until we entered Chesapeake Bay with zero visibility. Our radar, GPS, and AIS kept us on track and situationally aware but there were other boats that were seemingly lost and cruising around in circles. We made a point of tracking them on radar and occasionally making course corrections to avoid them. In the afternoon, the fog did eventually dissipate, and we found a snug anchorage with some new friends in a sailboat we had met in the Great Dismal Swamp.

Excerpts from Jill's Sketch Journal:

2/2–2/11 St. Augustine - Mooring right next to the Castillo de San Marcos meant taking in the views of the fort and the old city at all times of the day and night. Very dramatic. This was a great place to linger and explore. The water taxi was helpful on a couple of windy days when the dinghy ride would have been wet. This may be the oldest marina in the USA, who knows. The St. Augustine Municipal Marina is a treasure as it is right in the nation's oldest city, next to the Bridge of Lions. So much history here!

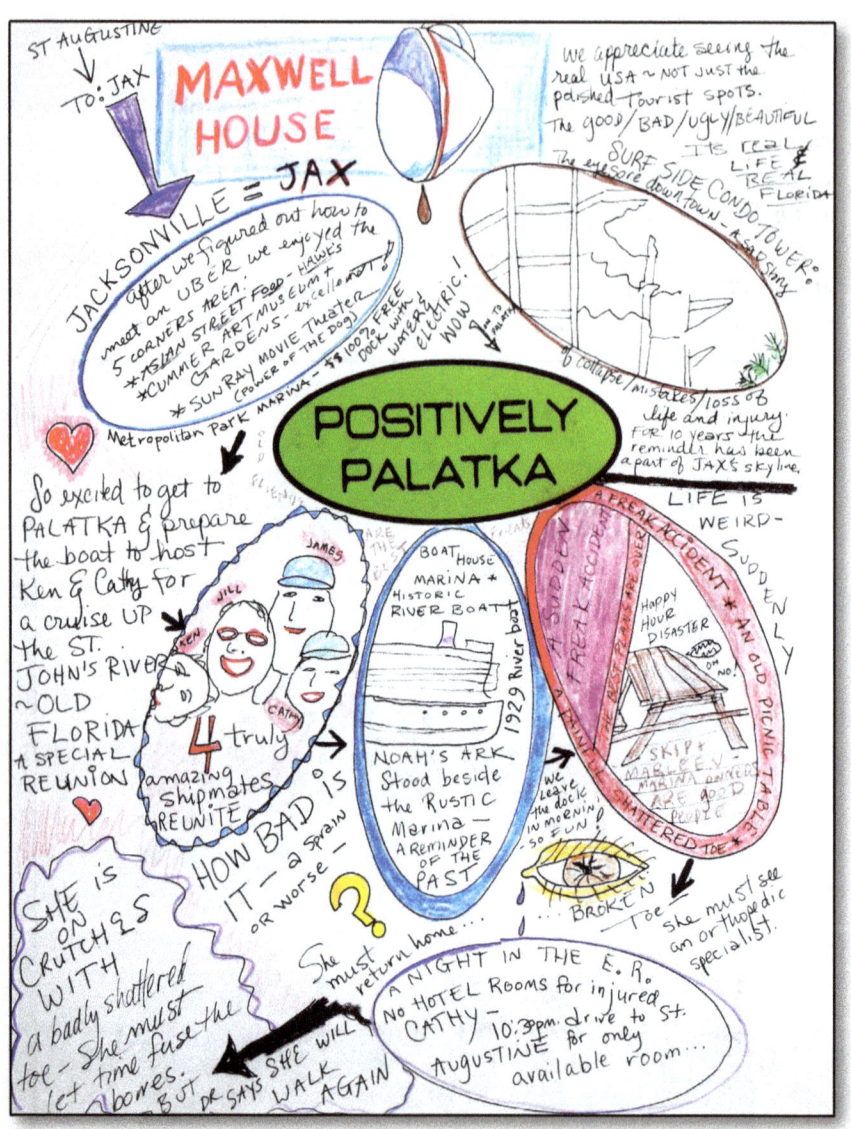

 2/13 From St. Augustine we moved on to Jacksonville. I read about the St. Johns River and had a family member that lived nearby some years ago. He was a bird lover and told me it was a prime location. A new part of Florida to explore that was described as "Old Florida" sounded like a great place to investigate and rest a bit while waiting for the right season to move north. It took us a while to find a walkable historic area in Jacksonville. It was a short Uber ride to the 5 Corners area and the Cummer Art Museum, restaurants, and a cool movie theater.

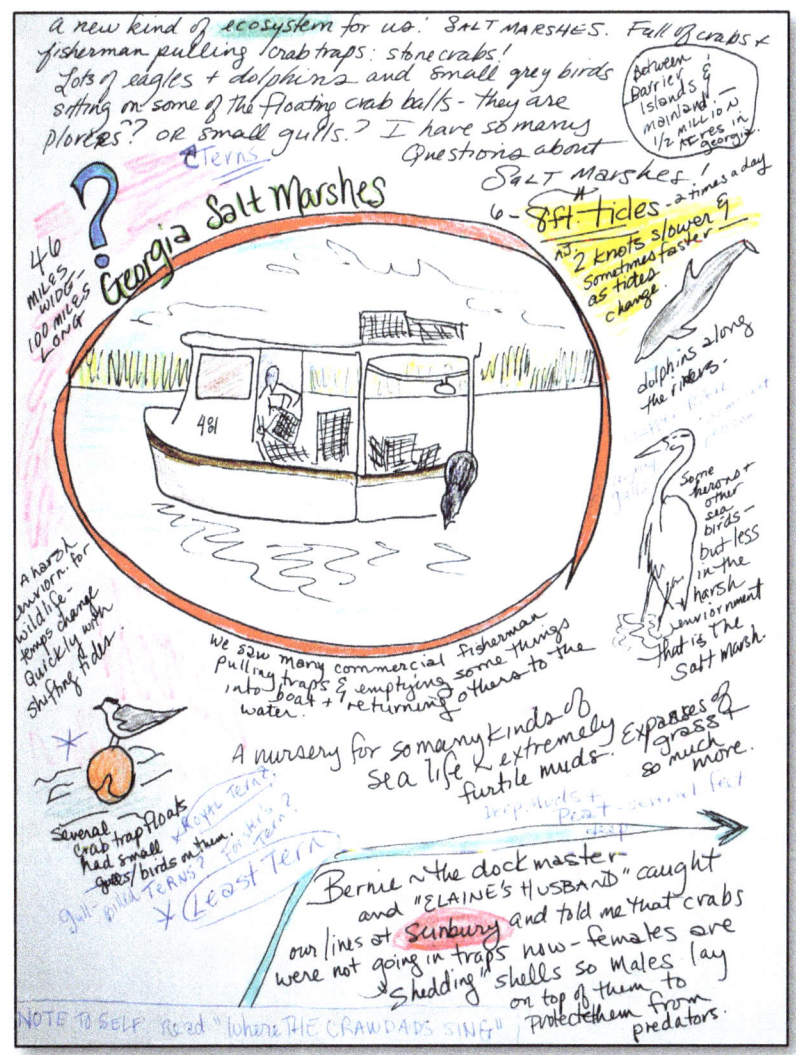

Back on the Alvin James we could see a huge "MAXWELL HOUSE, good to the last drop" mural painted on a building. Loved it!

2/17 We left Jacksonville and started our way up the St. Johns River. The town of Palatka and the Boat House Marina was our first stop, an old river town to walk around while we awaited the arrival of our oldest and closest cruising friends to join us for a week-long river cruise. I made butter chicken for our first night on the boat and we did some exploring of the town. The kind local boaters suggested we all meet at the picnic tables on the dock for a drink and to learn of their local river knowledge before our departure. Tragedy struck when the

table broke and smashed our dear friend's foot. After many hours in the emergency room, we learned this was a pretty serious injury that might require surgery. So, concerned and upset, we helped our friends pack up their gear to drive back home that very night. Safety on the boat is something James and I talked about often and over the years we have known many cruisers being injured aboard. We have heard of loopers breaking bones and having other medical emergencies. Besides being very prudent we could not protect our dear friend from a freak accident like this. It was with heavy hearts we left Palatka and moved up the river.

2/22 St. Johns River - Anchored on the river behind Hontoon Island. Eerie at anchor. Spanish moss, Cypress, so many birds, and many alligators. Decided to stay a second night to observe. Saw an alligator's red eyes in the spotlight and the creature seemed to move towards us. Limpkins screaming is like nothing I have ever heard! Purple gallinule, cattle egrets, many types of herons, and huge wood storks. Otherworldly!

2/24 – 16 days in Sanford. The slow boat ride from Hontoon Island to Sanford was absolutely spectacular! We lucked out and got a great slip in Monroe Harbor in Sanford – our own tropical 'Rear Window' off the stern with views of passing alligators, manatees, and people strolling in the park. Also coots, mallards, limpkins, giant catfish, turtles, ospreys, ibis, and many other varieties of birds. The metal roof over our slip kept us comfy as temperatures went over 80. We got some teak work and boat washing done. What a charming town with great festivals, restaurants, and Old Florida culture. S.L.O. Dancer caught up with us and we had more good times together.

oriental, n.c. is a happy place

..at free dock we had 3 people come to offer a ride to shop — two dozen came by to welcome us!

3/31/22 It was time to leave Florida for another kind of adventure and to move away from approaching heat — winter is over. Cumberland Island with wild horses and armadillos and the Carnegie mansion. Salt marshes — a new ecosystem to observe. Anchoring and watching the tides and changing landscape was so interesting. Docked at the Sunbury Crab Company. Very rustic — great vibe & so fun. High school prom kids in tuxes and formals arrive in a stretched

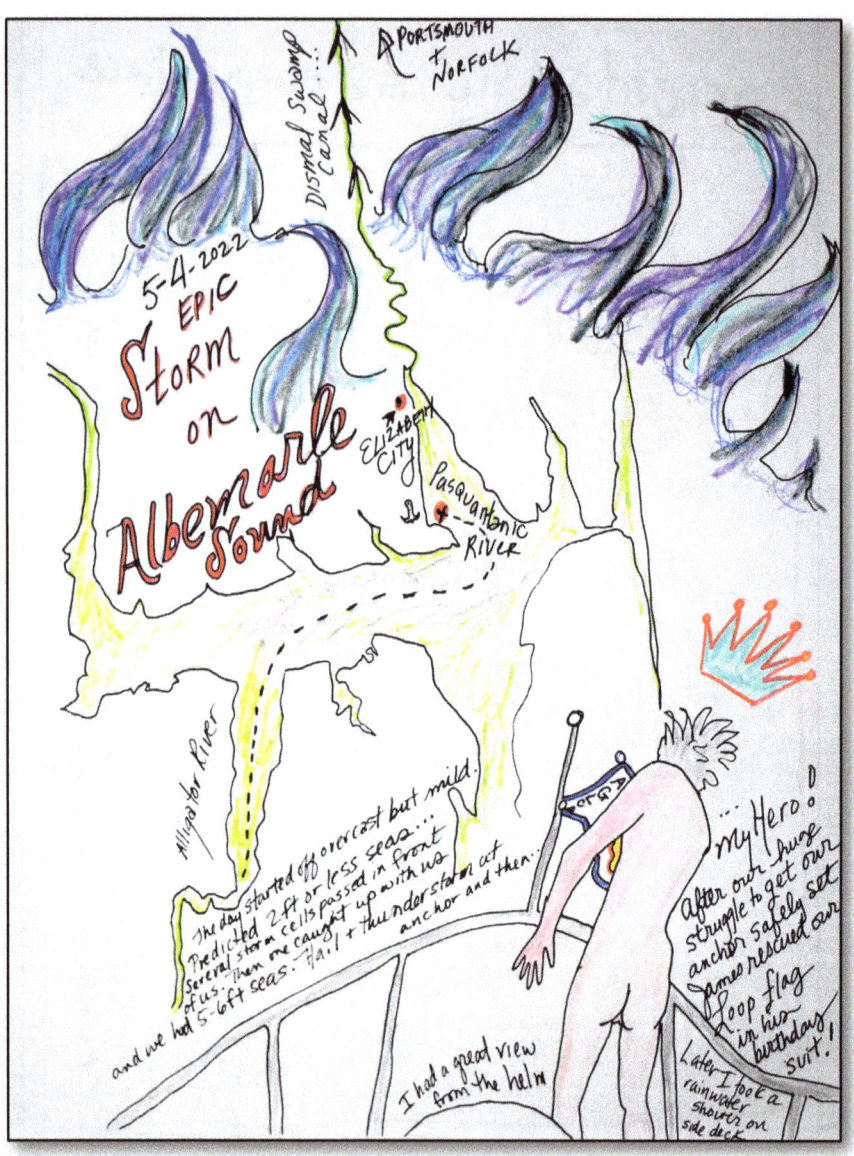

limo, sitting on worn benches. Peacocks strutting outside. Acres of marsh grasses! What is this world? Laid back charm.

    4/1 Brunswick, Georgia. Lots of wind but free beer and laundry at the marina. Birthplace of the shrimping industry. McClellanville & Beaufort, South Carolina mean lots of history and kindness. So much Southern charm. Jolly times were had at local "dive" bars with fellow loopers.

Squall on Albemarle Sound, on 5.4.2022

4/2 Sunbury Crab Company was a unique stop, docking in the salt marshes with wild peacocks, local kids in formal Prom attire in the open-air rustic crab shack, and watching the huge tides lift us up and down.

4/8 Beaufort, South Carolina another amazing historic small town. Georgetown, South Carolina is another town we must return to one day.

4/21 Beaufort, North Carolina. James turns 72. A week at the dock in Beaufort with visits from our friends Cathy (on crutches) and Ken and the crew of Sabot. Wild horses, beach walking, maritime history, and shrimp dinners.

5/1 Oriental, North Carolina. Free dock. Friendliest town ever! Three different groups of locals stopped to say hello and offer rides to grocery shops. Charming streets to walk. 1,000 residents and 3,000 boats! Met Fae, a 100-year-old resident and athlete! Was inspired by the surroundings and stories to do several pages about Oriental.

5/3 Belhaven, North Carolina, The mayor, Ricky Credle, pulled his truck over to welcome us to town and just to say hello as we strolled around the town.

5/4 Albemarle Sound. The day started off mild with seas two feet or less. A day we couldn't have planned for – a skill building day – a few minutes of terror we will remember. We have had a handful of these kinds of experiences as

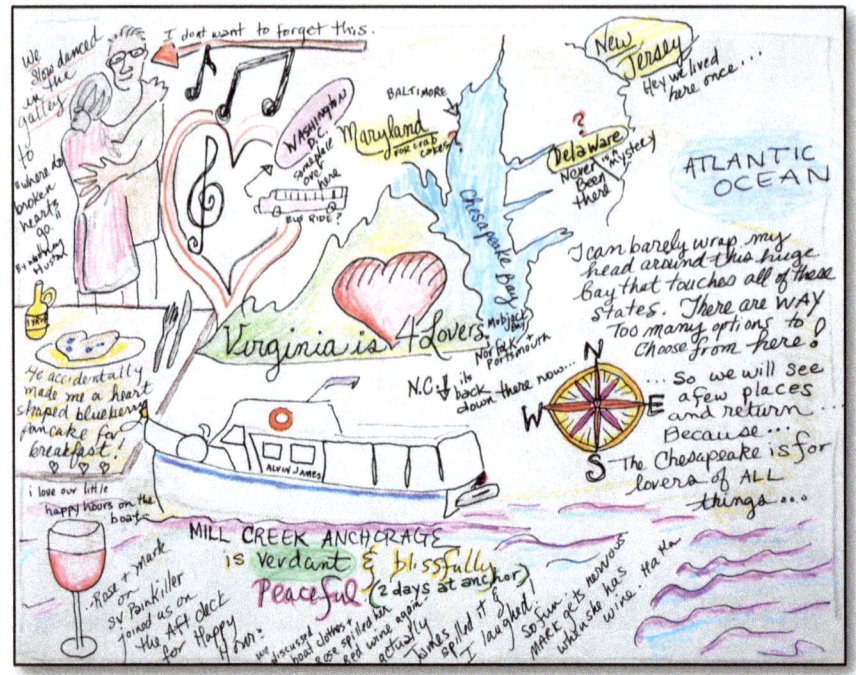

cruisers, we try to avoid them but we always know this can happen and we use all our skills, senses, and our fortitude to get through them. "Courage is resistance to fear, mastery of fear, not absence of fear" Mark Twain.

5/5 Elizabeth City free docks and quick exploring of a very interesting town.

5/6 The Great Dismal Swamp connects Albemarle Sound with the Chesapeake. It is so green and restful. Saw turtles, nutria, songbirds, and snapping turtles. Thought about the enslaved people who dug this canal by hand in 1805. It was also a hideout for those traveling on the Underground Railroad.

5/7 Norfolk and Portsmouth, Virginia. Spent a week waiting for a Nor'easter to pass.

5/16 A few foggy days after the storm subsided and it was on to the Chesapeake Bay. In the Deltaville Marina we met 'Bob 423' whose trail we followed up the ICW. He asked for directions to the laundry room, and we directed him! A nice guy and his wife is a pastel and oil painting artist aboard their boat. Cool! Pizza on the veranda with the crews of three Island Packet sailboats. One of them, Mark and Rose from Painkiller, we had met back in our Wisconsin hometown. The cruising community is so small and tight knit.

78 • *Exploring America's Great Loop*

5/18 Home – The word means sanctuary, a safe spot. But is doesn't have to be straight walls and stillness. It can be a 33-ft. vessel that knows no boundaries and can still be our safe nest. Nice passage to Mill's Creek where we spent 2 calm days at anchor next to Painkiller. Potluck meals and board games.

To New York and the Canals

*Being on a boat that's moving through the water, it's so clear.
Everything falls into place in terms of what's important and what's not.*

James Taylor

We were happy to have made it to Chesapeake Bay, a legendary cruising ground. The bay is studded with islands and rivers creating countless protected anchorages to spend a day or two swimming, fishing, or just enjoying being on the water. Our next stop was the Deltaville marina, chosen for its convivial reputation and the fact that it was within walking or biking distance of a West Marine store. We had broken a boat hook and needed a replacement. We managed to get to the marina well in advance of a storm that arrived later with much sound and fury. It signified nothing however because we were able to watch it from the veranda of the clubhouse overlooking our boat which was securely tied to the dock. The next day dawned warm and sunny, and we bicycled to West Marine and bought the boat hook. I hadn't realized that bicycling back to *Alvin James* with a 6-foot-long boat hook might present a problem. I managed to tuck it under my arm and point it out in front of me like some medieval knight in a jousting competition.

Leaving Deltaville in the morning, we continued north on the bay to a beautiful, sheltered anchorage known locally as Mill Creek. We swam and explored the area in our dinghy. We walked the beach of a deserted island until we were driven away by the ferocious residents (mosquitoes!) and retreated back to our boat. We needed fuel so at sunrise we left for the town of Solomons, Maryland.

Solomons is a water-oriented town with many marinas, waterfront establishments, and a wonderful maritime museum. We got a slip at the Solomons Yachting Center. Getting around on foot was very inconvenient so we commuted everywhere in our dinghy.

That evening, I had the best crab cakes I had ever eaten. Expensive, but so sublime they were worth the price. In the morning we dinghied over to the museum which had a wonderful collection of classic watercraft and a screwpile lighthouse to tour.

I used the marina's Wi-Fi connection to download the novel *"Chesapeake"* by James Michener. Like most of Michener's books, it's about as big as an old Sears catalogue (remember those?) but the digital version on my Kindle could be held in one hand. It was superbly researched and filled with details that added immensely to my enjoyment of the trip.

After Solomons we continued north stopping at Herrington Harbour and Deale before crossing to the east side of the bay and St. Michaels Island, home of the Chesapeake Bay Maritime Museum. The museum is a large campus with many buildings and docks full of historic boats. It also offers docking facilities for transient boaters. All slips had been reserved but we were fortunate that bad weather had delayed the arrival of one boat, and we were offered the space. The harbor master suspected the other boat would probably not arrive for three more days and if we wished to stay longer when the other boar arrived we could just anchor out nearby. Since there was a discounted rate on slip rentals for museum members we became members, and it just so happened that there were several catered events that weekend for members. So not only were we able to stay at the discounted rate, but we also ate and drank quite well at the galas. The town of St. Michaels is right outside the gates of the museum and is also a great place to explore. After we were notified that we had to vacate the slip, we just motored about fifty yards offshore and dropped the hook. We had access to the museum grounds and the town via our dinghy and there was even a pump-out service that came out to our anchored boat.

Voyage Log #16
Dear Friends and Shipmates,

Waiting out bad weather is what prudent crews do when traveling. Aboard Alvin James we make go/no go decisions together. Either of us can veto the decision to leave port based on our comfort level with the marine forecast. We stayed a week in Portsmouth waiting out a Nor'easter that was battering the east coast. When we finally left port, we were surprised by heavy fog that descended on us as we entered Chesapeake Bay. With our radar, AIS transponder, and chart plotter we felt confident in our ability to avoid trouble and find a safe anchorage for the night. We did manage to avoid two pleasure boats that appeared to be lost and were appearing out of the mist every so often going in a different direction with each encounter. That night, we anchored out in idyllic Mobjack Bay. Next day we spent several days in Deltaville before moving on to North Beach. We crossed the bay to Saint Michaels and are moored at the Chesapeake Bay Maritime Museum. Four days tied up to a dock while a cold front with lots of rain moved over, then dropped anchor about a hundred yards off the dock as the sun and warm weather returned. We are fortunate to be here for the Memorial Day weekend. Lots of activities on the museum grounds with free food and drinks for members! Yes, we became members. Our plans are very fluid but in the next few weeks we will cross from the Chesapeake to the Delaware River and then up the New Jersey coast to New York city.

Stay healthy. Stay in touch.

We next crossed back over to the west side of the bay to visit Annapolis. Known as a great sailing town and the home of the U.S. Naval Academy, Annapolis was high on our list of places to visit. We got a mooring ball just a short hop from the dinghy dock and planned our exploration. The issue being, it was just too damned hot and humid! Walking on the streets we would look for scraps of shade to escape the broiling sun. Our boat has no air conditioning and became an oven during the day. If we weren't ashore seeking refuge in some air-conditioned spot, we sat in front of fans on the boat. The harbor was too dirty and busy to swim in so there was no escape until the sun dipped below the horizon and life became bearable again. As much as the town appealed to us, we cut our visit short and headed north to Baltimore, Maryland.

The Fells Point neighborhood in Baltimore is very cool with lots to see and do. Adding to its charm was the fact that an old friend from Chicago had moved to the area 30 years ago and offered to be our guide. The weather had moderated a bit, so it was more pleasant to stroll around the historic streets and, since we were at a marina, we had plenty of shore power to run fans on the boat. If your only experience of Baltimore is watching Fox News or "The Wire" you might think of the city as a crime-ridden hellscape. I'm sure there are parts of the city that deserve that description, but our week-long stay revealed a vibrant urban culture full of art, music, good food, and much to see and do.

Leaving Baltimore, it took us two days to work our way to the top of the bay and through the C&D Canal to Delaware City, located on the west bank of the Delaware River just north of the point it widens into the estuary of Delaware Bay. The bay is another one of those bodies of water that has a cranky reputation compounded by the fact that there are few safe places to bail out if things get ugly. The harbormaster at the Delaware City Marina is a knowledgeable old pro who hosts a nightly briefing for boaters hoping to transit the bay south to Cape May, New Jersey. He went over the latest weather models and tide tables with the captains and crews of boats waiting to depart and predicted that our best chance for a drama-free crossing would be in two days. Leaving at 7:00 a.m. would give us five hours of favorable tide and very little in the way of wind driven waves. We followed his advice and arrived in Cape May unscathed. We anchored in Cape May Harbor after being informed that there would be no slip available for us until the next day. The following day we tied up at the South Jersey Marina in Cape May for a two-day stay.

Cape May is a beautiful oceanside resort community that has been a summer retreat since the 1800s. Most boaters heading to New York City and points north from Cape May opt for the outside route on the Atlantic Ocean. The New Jersey Intracoastal Waterway has not been regularly dredged and is terrifyingly shallow in spots. There are many bridges that require opening and New Jersey boaters have a reputation for inconsiderate behavior. If the conditions on the ocean are benign, the outside route is the wiser option. However, the Atlantic Ocean was not in a cooperative mood with gusty winds and high waves. Best predictions for calmer conditions looked like four days away. Jill and I wanted to get going so we did our due diligence on the inside route. I compiled a list of bridges that required opening with locations and contact info. I also charted notoriously shallow sections and timed our departure to traverse them on a rising tide.

We were confident we had done our homework when we left the dock at 8:00 a.m. At 9:10 a.m. we were aground in the channel about six miles north of Cape May! It was three hours till high tide, so we dropped the anchor to prevent the current from making our situation worse and waited for the incoming tide to hopefully lift us off. Sure enough, several hours later I was able to start the engine and back our almost floating boat out of the embrace of dark gooey mud and back into navigable water. We continued, not quite as confident but wiser. We anchored for the night about 20 miles south of Atlantic City. The winds that were making for hazardous conditions on the ocean were felt in our anchorage, but the lack of fetch meant the water was flat. We had a very peaceful night.

Retrieving the anchor against a strong wind in the morning was a trick that required close coordination between the person on the anchor windlass (me) and the helmsperson (Jill). I managed to jam the chain in the windlass, and it took a partial disassembly and reassembly to get things right. It took a bit more time than expected but soon we were on our way. The approaches to Atlantic City became more urban with a densely populated shore featuring lots of seawalls, docks, and boats. We reserved a slip at the Golden Nugget Casino Marina. We took a walk on the famous boardwalk but returned to the boat needing a bit of peace and quiet. No such luck! The casino was hosting a very loud concert and thousands of people were being their loud, happy, drunken selves. We placed an order online through a grocery delivery service. We were assured our order would be delivered to the marina in one hour. Two hours later, a stressed out and confused driver arrived and told us horror stories about the near impossibility of negotiating the traffic around the concert site. We gave her a generous tip and took our bags to the boat only to discover we were missing some items, and some substitutions were made with other items someone (not us!) considered a close match. Lesson learned. Oh, almost forgot, there was no hot water available in the marina washrooms.

We were happy to leave and be on our way. After another anchorage, we spent our last night on the New Jersey Intracoastal Waterway at the Bay Head Yacht Club, where we anchored just off the club's docks and were greeted by the harbormaster and several members who wished us a pleasant stay and offered us any help that might be needed. At sunrise, we motored out of the Manasquan Inlet into the Atlantic Ocean for a 40-mile offshore trip to Highlands, New Jersey. Highlands is sheltered by the imposing spit of Sandy Hook and the high bluffs of the town are dominated by the unusual Twin Lights lighthouse. We booked a slip at the Twin Lights Marina and stayed for several days reacquainting ourselves with the Jersey Shore and visiting a dear old friend. We had a great reunion and caught up on things after being apart for more than 30 years.

Our marina in Highlands offered a view of the Verrazzano-Narrows Bridge marking the entrance to New York Harbor. The morning we left was gray and misty and the distinctive skyline of New York City did not appear until we had passed under the bridge. Commercial boats, towboats with barges, tour boats, and ferries churned the waters with their wakes. Soon the distinctive green color of Lady Liberty became visible against a backdrop of skyscrapers. My charts indicated a likely area to drop anchor between the exclusion zone immediately around the statue and the navigation channels farther out. Jill motored slowly into a spot a short distance from the statue and close to Ellis Island. When the depth sounder indicated the fifteen feet we were looking for, she stopped the boat's forward progress and gave me the signal to release the anchor. After letting out a generous amount of chain and making sure we were secure, we spent some time looking around at our spectacular surroundings. The beautiful and iconic statue was right out our front window and the buildings of our country's largest city all around us. The parade of traffic continued unabated, roiling the water into a steady chop, but as night began to fall and the boat traffic slowed things became still and peaceful. The lights of Manhattan began to wink on, and the city looked like a film set we had seen countless times in movies over the decades. Some friends had given us a bottle of champagne as a going-away gift to celebrate a special occasion. Jill had the foresight to put it in the refrigerator early in the day and we popped the cork, poured it into flutes with strawberries and celebrated this milestone of our trip. We put on music and danced on the aft deck, savoring this special moment we had accomplished together.

Voyage Log #17
Friends and Shipmates,

We finished our cruise up the Chesapeake with a wonderful visit with old friends in Baltimore. Our marina was pretty rustic but was located in the neighborhood of Fells Point. We found it to be charming, filled with 19th-century row houses on cobblestone streets and many restaurants and taverns. After several days enjoying our urban adventure, we traveled to the top of the bay and through the C&D canal to Delaware City where we prepared for a trip down Delaware Bay to Cape May, New Jersey. Delaware Bay has a strong tidal current and very few places to bail out if things get rough. Strong winds opposing the tidal flow create very nasty conditions. The harbormaster in Delaware City gave a daily weather briefing and advised us that the following day would be the best opportunity to make a dash down the bay. His prediction proved right, and we had a drama-free trip to Cape May.

 Arriving in Cape May, the boater intending to travel to New York Harbor faces a choice: go outside and travel the entire Jersey coast on the Atlantic Ocean or stay on the New Jersey Intracoastal Waterway all the way to Manasquan, where a short 40-mile ocean passage is required to enter New York Harbor. Both have advantages and disadvantages. The 170-mile open ocean trip has plenty of deep water and few obstacles to avoid. The disadvantage is strong winds can create a sea state ranging from uncomfortable to dangerous. Those considering this option must wait for a window of at least twenty-four hours of settled weather. The Intracoastal option is longer and slower and has sections so shallow that they should only be attempted on a rising tide. Conditions in the wind-whipped Atlantic meant staying put for at least four days so we decided to do the inside route. Before leaving, I made a list of all bridges and which ones required openings. We also made a point of only traveling on favorable tides. Well, within two hours of leaving Cape May we found ourselves aground on a mud bank and unable to extricate ourselves! So, we waited about an hour and a half for the tide to gently lift us off and we continued on our way. This proved to be the only time we touched bottom. That evening, we anchored in a salt marsh and enjoyed watching people fishing and digging for clams. Next day we traveled to Atlantic City. We stayed at a marina adjacent to and managed by the Golden Nugget casino. We took a shuttle to the boardwalk, a prime location for people watching! Returning to the boat, Jill made a grocery order from a food delivery service. Hours later, after many dropped phone calls and texts, the person with our order arrived amid all the confusion in front of the Golden Nugget and across the street from a live concert on the marina deck. Back on the boat, we discovered some items missing and others substituted with items we didn't want. Lesson: having your groceries delivered to a casino is not a sure bet.

 We anchored two more nights before leaving the Manasquan inlet and into the Atlantic. We entered New York Harbor and got a slip in Highlands, New Jersey, in sight of the Verrazzano-Narrows Bridge. We will visit with an old friend from our Jersey days before anchoring out by the Statue of Liberty. I am glad to get the Atlantic Ocean behind us and start our trek through New York to the Great Lakes.

Stay well my friends.

At dawn, we got underway and cruised up the Hudson as the beauty of New York City dissolved seamlessly into the natural beauty of the Palisades on the Hudson River. We stopped at the Half Moon Bay Marina in the village of Croton-on-Hudson. We planned to spend several days exploring Manhattan and did not wish to pay the extortionist rates at city marinas. Our chosen marina was a healthy walk from the commuter train that would take us right into Grand Central Station. We traveled to the city two days in a row and had a memorable time. So much to see and do. Definitely a highlight of our trip.

With our itch for an urban experience well-scratched, we continued through the forested mountains of the Hudson River Valley for several days until just past Troy, New Jersey, we turned off the Hudson onto the Mohawk River to Waterford, New York, and the start of the Erie Canal.

Voyage Log #18
Friends and Shipmates,

Though I often write about the sea, I would never harbor the conceit that I am in the company of Melville or Homer. Yet sometimes I feel I walk in their footsteps. Yesterday as we left Troy, New York, I could not help but think of Odysseus and his long, eventful journey to return home from Troy. No Cyclops or Calypso stands in my way, and we should touch our home shore in less than the 10 years it took Odysseus.

As I write this, we are at a free dock just outside the first lock of the Erie Canal. We have already transited the Federal Lock on the Hudson River that marks the end of the Hudson tidal estuary. That means for the rest of our trip, we will be in tideless fresh water!

We hope to be on the shores of Lake Ontario next week and will prep for a crossing into Canada. The weather is getting hot and humid here and the thought of cool, clean Canadian waters is most inviting. Swimming off our anchored boat is a pleasure that we have enjoyed only occasionally on this trip. Polluted water or dangerous sea life rule out swimming in many areas. Our Great Lakes are special, let's not forget it.

One final note: there is a 35-foot boat tied up next to us at the Waterford free dock. It belongs to an older couple in their 80s who have completed the Great

Loop 33 times! Yes, they have been in continuous circulation, traveling from harbor to harbor visiting old friends and making new ones for 33 years!

They have been doing this for more than three decades! A different life choice for sure!

Be safe, healthy, and happy!

The eastern terminus of the Erie Canal is at Waterford, New York. We tied up along the wall with about a dozen other vessels preparing for their Erie Canal adventure. The city is home to a visitors center and is in sight of the first lock, mysteriously named Lock 2. The visitors center was also playing host to a steamboat festival and a section of the wall was reserved for them. Steamboat aficionados are a rare and eccentric breed of boaters who were friendly and enthusiastic about introducing novices into their world where the romantic technology of the 19th century is celebrated. Jill and I accepted invitations to cruise up and down the river on one of the craft and the next day, when friends came to visit us, we took another excursion. I was amazed at how quiet the steam engines were, more like a sewing machine than the rumble of *Alvin James*'s diesel engine. I also tried calculating the cost of fuel difference. The price of diesel fuel was at an all-time high and the scrap wood burned by the steamboats seemed pretty cheap.

Our trip through the canal was an enjoyable cruise through history. We took advantage of the many free walls and docks to stay at overnight and spent less money on this leg of the trip than any other. The lack of commercial traffic made lock transits fast and pleasurable. After the welcoming town of Phoenix, we left the Erie Canal system and turned onto the Oswego canal for a twenty-mile jaunt to Oswego, New York, on the shore of Lake Ontario. We were back in the Great Lakes and had three of these inland seas to cross before we were home. The marina in Oswego was filled with boats, some loopers, some not, prepping for crossing Lake Ontario. Having heard that fuel in Canada was 10 dollars a gallon we topped our tanks with relatively cheap stateside diesel. A good weather window for a lake crossing looked to be a couple of days away so we spent the time enjoying the town. We were befriended by the crews of two boats with no Great Lakes experience and were nervous about a big open water passage. They peppered us with questions about where on the other side of the lake we planned to stay and when we planned to depart. Finally, they asked if they could just tag along. Since our boats all had similar cruising speeds, it seemed like no imposition, so we agreed. On the appointed day we left the confines of the canals we had traveled on for weeks and entered the vast water world of Lake Ontario with its limitless watery horizon spreading out in front of us. Our little armada fell dutifully in line behind us, and we plowed over smooth seas under a cloudless blue sky toward the Canadian shore. Six hours later, we anchored in Prinyer Cove and cleared Canadian customs by phone. It felt so good to be back in Canada after having been locked out for two years because of Covid restrictions. The North Channel of Lake Huron is our preferred cruising ground, and we have many Canadian friends we had not seen in years. Though we had never been in this part of Canada it felt like we were in home waters.

Voyage Log #19
Friends and Shipmates,

There comes a time in every voyage where one's thoughts turn to the end. After transiting the Erie and Oswego canals, and arriving on the southern shore of Lake Ontario, I have begun to anticipate the end of this great adventure. Ahead of us are crossings of the inland seas and a serpentine journey across the Trent-Severn Waterway. There are many weeks of challenges to come but the thought of home is an undeniable pleasure.

There is a natural process where lived experiences becomes memories. Our memories are imbued with little fictions that become our life stories. My stories will be filled with places and dates, with the serendipity of discovering like-minded souls, and the sweet sadness of many goodbyes. The charming towns along the way and the great bodies of water that in turn could be tranquil, beautiful, or ominous. Jill and I will return to the life we led before. We will take up where we left off with our family and our beloved friends. The old familiar routines of living along the lake in Manitowoc will be a comfort. But I am sure that looking out my kitchen window at that beautiful expanse of Lake Michigan will rekindle memories of the year I spent with Jill on this great adventure.

Stay healthy, be happy. See you soon.

In the morning we traveled to the town of Trenton which is the gateway to the extensive canal system known as the Trent-Severn Waterway. Incorporating 44 locks it cuts across Ontario and empties into Lake Huron's Georgian Bay at the Town of Severn. The locks on the Trent-Severn are a joy. Most are nestled in beautiful manicured parklike settings with plenty of wall space above and below the lock chambers to tie up for a leisurely lunch or an overnight stay. The attendants are mostly college-age kids who are competent and unfailingly polite. Many of the locks are operated by hand-cranked turnstiles powered by the attendants. Three of the locks on the system are worthy of note. The Peterborough and Kirkfield locks are hydraulic lift locks, the only ones in North America. When the gates open, boats enter large pans of water, and the entire pan is raised to the next level. The Big Chute Marine Railway is a huge, motorized platform that rides on rails into the water, boats are floated onto it and strapped into place. The platform then reverses course, rising out of the water, up a hill, over a road and down the other side of the hill into the water where the boats are floated off and continue on their way.

The whole waterway is punctuated by charming little towns and beautiful scenery. We spent about 2½ weeks motoring the 240-mile length of the waterway before entering Georgian Bay.

Voyage Log #20
Friends and Shipmates,

Recently we transited the last lock in our journey. The Port Severn lock is the last lock on the western terminus of the Trent-Severn Waterway that crosses Ontario and empties into Lake Huron's Georgian Bay. The first lock on our trip was the Chicago River lock that allows boats to pass from Lake Michigan into downtown Chicago and to the great Midwest rivers (Illinois, Mississippi, Ohio, and Tennessee). One hundred and six locks on the route we chose. Lake Michigan is 579 feet above sea level. Heading from our home in Manitowoc to the Gulf of Mexico the locks had to lower us a total of 579 feet. Then after traveling at sea level along the gulf and Atlantic coasts, we traveled through locks raising us back up to the level of Lake Michigan. From the huge industrial locks of America's heartland that swallow barges and tows 600 feet long and 100 feet wide to Canadian locks still powered by human muscle turning cranks to open and close gates. There were two hydraulic lift locks where we drove our boat into a giant water-filled tub that was then lifted 60 feet in the air where we would exit into the canal's new level. And most unusual of all was the Big Chute Marine Railway, where an enormous rail car rode tracks into the water. Boats floated over it, and after being secured with straps, were carried over a hill and deposited in the water on the other side. Lockmasters and other employees represented the best of public servants: knowledgeable, helpful, and unfailingly friendly.

Now we are on Lake Huron which is the same level as Lake Michigan. No more locks between here and home.

Stay healthy. Hope to see you soon.

Excerpts from Jill's Sketch Journal:

5/20 Then up the Chesapeake to Maryland. Maryland is a state we have never visited – "The Land of Pleasant Living" had so much to offer! Solomons. Yikes! It's 96 degrees! We explore by dinghy, it's a watery world.

5/24 St. Michaels, Maryland. A slip at the fantastic Chesapeake Maritime Museum where we feel we are part of an exhibit as we are on the Waterman's

Shack dock. A fabulous experience. We had full access to this amazing museum campus. I woke early to sketch the building of the Maryland Dove schooner. We became members of the museum and attended 2 'members only' events. Walked downtown, ate amazing crab cakes, and observed an osprey nesting and living on a piling in the marina.

6/3–6/10 Baltimore, Maryland - Henderson's Wharf Marina, historic Fell's Point. At the suggestion of an old friend originally from Chicago, we visited Baltimore, and we were so glad we did! Having Brian and Iris to show us around and tell us what we had to see made it an excellent stop on our loop.

So many highlights: Bertha's Mussels — excellent food and live music, Visionary Art Museum — Great Art and Captain Crunch French Toast at local eatery, Black Crowned Night Herons — Nesting in Thames Park. Wow! Water Taxi — Fun way to get around. Walking cobblestone streets and seeing historic row houses. Harbor views — great sketching opportunities, the Ministry of Brewing.

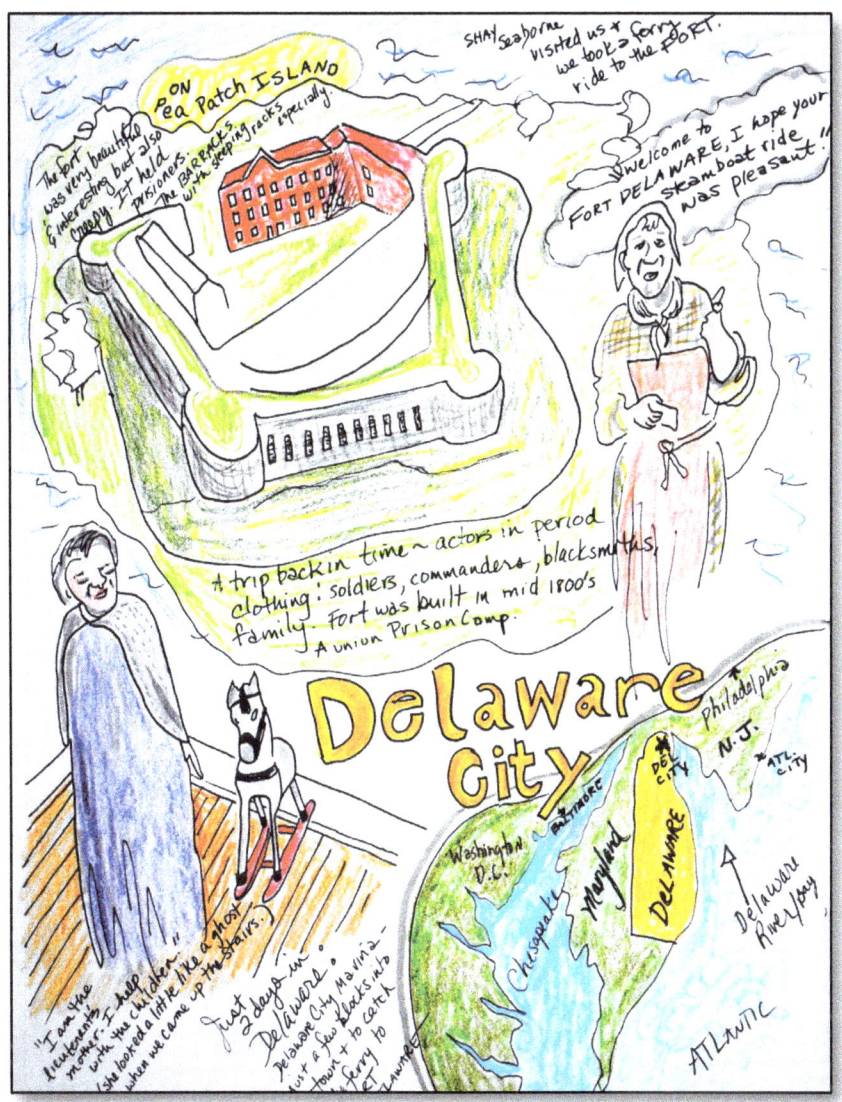

6/11 Delaware City - Shay, a new friend, joined us and acted as tour guide to Fort Delaware and Pea Patch Island. An historic trip back in time.

6/13 Cape May, New Jersey. - We stopped to rest, putting our anchor down next to the only USCG training center in the country. Heard the reveille and retreat bugle and the sound of training platoons marching and calling cadence. Brought back lots of memories of my Army time. Observing life from an anchorage is always a sweet treat. After a nights rest we moved on to the South Jersey Marina which was very tight with two 60 to 70-ft. boats moving out as we

moved in. James' boat handling skills are so good and our communication skills are great so we did just fine. Cape May calls itself the first resort town in the USA. Beautiful Victorian homes! We took in a play by a local theater group. Three days later we are moving on, James studied the Jersey ICW and decided that we could take it despite warning of shallow depths. The outside ocean passage is out of the question because of high winds. So off we go with strategies to deal with the shallows using the tides to our advantage. Alas, we were aground for several hours until the rising tide floated us off. That night we observed a

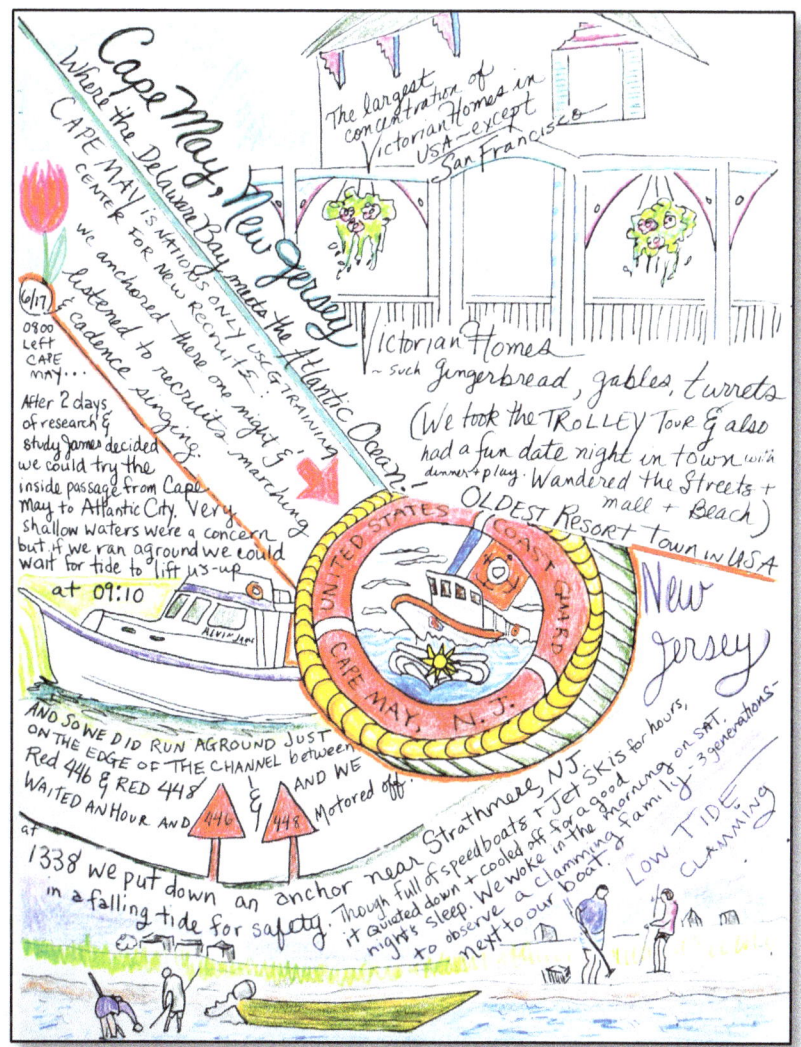

three-generation family clamming where we anchored. I love watching life from our home, it's always changing.

6/18 Atlantic City, New Jersey - A real slice of life. We walked the boardwalk, took some public transportation, and finally ordered groceries using Instacart and had a 10:40 p.m. delivery to the casino we were docked at. Not our favorite stop but observing life adds to the adventure. We find things to see everywhere we go.

6/19 More Jersey ICW, playing the tides. James studies the tide tables and we very carefully stay in the channels. No rush, easy going, safety first.

6/20 Anchored in front of Bayhead Yacht Club and "Buddy" came out to welcome us. Several boaters came by in dinghies to say hello as we prepared supper and read and rested.

6/22 Twin Lights Marina, Highlands, New Jersey. Steve and Marie don't get a lot of transients in their marina we assume...people skills are not their strong point, but we are safe and comfortable. Enjoyed walking up to the Twin Lights lighthouse, a good workout on a long uphill climb. Old friend, John Shea came to our boat, and we took him to dinner. He chose the very historic Bahr's Restaurant where the Soprano's prequel was filmed. We really enjoyed walking around the neighborhoods here.

6/23 New York City! A very exciting short run from Highlands, past Sandy Hook, Verrazzano Narrows Bridge to the Statue of Liberty! Anchored between the Statue of Liberty and Ellis Island. Wow! Champagne and strawberries, toasts, and a dance with a few tears of happiness. Sure, it's a bit bumpy with ferries and boat traffic but a small price to pay for a fantastic night and morning watching the city.

6/24 Next, up the Hudson River to Half Moon Bay Marina, in Croton-on-Hudson. This was a good spot to affordably explore NYC using the MTA train to get to Grand Central Station. Day one in the Big Apple we experienced the Whitney Art Museum – fabulous! Enjoyed the High Line – An elevated city park: Repurposed elevated train tracks filled with lush gardens, sculpture, murals, city views, cafés, and wine bars. People watching is great! Day two in the Big Apple - Met a young couple, Abigail and Ceci, on the train dressed to the

nines and excited to attend their first Pride Fest! Rockefeller Center was decorated with rainbow flags and filled with fountains, roller skating, and thousands of people enjoying the beautiful day. We later walked to Central Park and took a Jitney ride with a kind and knowledgeable tour guide from West Africa named Check. He dropped us at the Guggenheim. Afterwards we stopped for coffee in a beautiful arched room in a spectacular Episcopalian Church – Blue Stone Lane Upper East Side Cafe – in the Church of Heavenly Rest. An aesthetic experience I won't soon forget. The sandstone arches of the cloistered space are superb. So many miles walked and so much experienced in two days in NYC!

6/28 Hudson River - Beautiful Hudson River Passage. Loved every minute of it. Low key day on the boat at Donovan's Shady Harbor Marina; grocery shopping with a courtesy car, laundry, and happy hour with fellow loopers.

6/30 Headed to the Erie Canal, a short day on the boat to Waterford, New York. Tying to the free wall at the visitor's center for three nights. We lucked out as we arrived just in time for a steamboat festival and fireworks! Ted and Sarah Pongracz docked behind us on a Kady Krogen Manatee. They have completed 31 Loops!!! Met steamboat captains and crews and took two fantastic rides on the Santana, a miniature steam tug built by Captain Larry.

A couple of friends, Charles and Lark, looked us up and joined us for a great time in Waterford, The gateway to the Erie Canal.

7/3 Left Waterford and did a flight of five locks. Tied up at a $20 a night dock in Scotia, New York. Enjoyed a local landmark, Jumpin' Jack's Drive-In. Met some new loopers and had a peaceful night. Loved seeing Dee Dee and John of War Eagle again!

7/5 A really nice city marina in Little Falls, New York. Quaint town with a food co-op! Cool library in a beautiful historic home.

7/6 I really felt the history of the Erie Canal, especially walking the tow path, the same place mules and horses pulled barges. The waterways of America were huge investments, and it took the work of so many to dig them. Quite astounding!

7/8 Sylvan Beach, New York Two nights on the town's free wall next to a very old amusement park. Got a fortune from Zoltar. Met the crew of Dirt Free, Sharon and Wallace. They are marine surveyors from Canada living aboard a perfect boat – a Benford Fantail 38 which they had lovingly restored.

7/9 Phoenix, New York is the home of Lock #1 on the Oswego Canal and home of the Bridgehouse Brats. So inspiring! Teaching the town's young people the value of cooperative community service and leadership. The free docks are beautifully maintained by a group of youngsters who welcome boaters and run

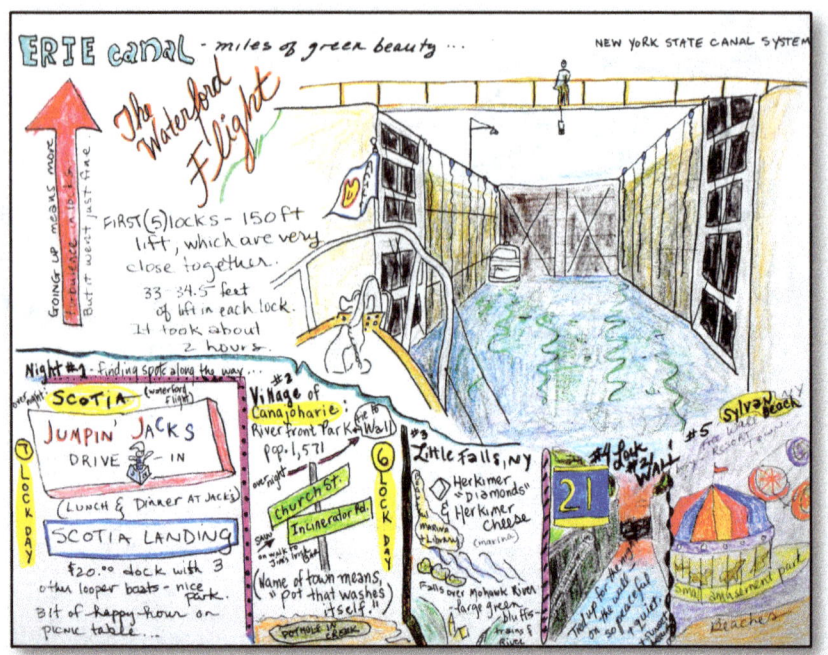

errands, wash boats, lend bikes, and pick up to-go meals from local restaurants – all for free! We tipped generously of course and left inspired by this radical hospitality.

7/10 To Lake Ontario - The Oswego Canal was beautiful! Seven locks in one day! Oswego Marina fuel dock – I fell off the boat between the dock and Alvin James trying to do a "too athletic" jump. Not badly injured except my pride. I swam to the stern and climbed up the swim ladder. A quick rinse in the shower and fresh clothes and I was fine. Once again I reflected on how fortunate we have been not to be sick or injured so far.

7/14 Crossing into Canada! We tied to a mooring ball in Prinyer Cove in Ontario, after an uneventful crossing of Lake Ontario. Cleared customs using our phone and we celebrated being back in Canada again. Finally! All the Canadian flags along the waterways made me feel so happy because I lived in Canada every summer until I was 21 years old, and because we visited Ontario as a couple for so many years. This is definitely a happy homecoming for me.

7/16 Starting the Trent Severn Canal. This historic canal has been on our wish list for years. So excited to experience this. This canal is a Canadian national treasure and a looper's delight!

7/17 Campbellford city wall - right next to the "giant toonie" - rainy day sketching and exploring.

7/19 At anchor in Rice Lake after a 90-degree day and 6 locks. We swam off the boat and the water felt amazing and healed the deer fly bites. Made sautéed vegetables and Salisbury Steak. We needed to cook as we had accidentally turned off the fridge and everything had defrosted.

7/20 Left our nice anchorage for Petersborough and only one lock to do – a welcome break! Two very different experiences today: solitude at anchor and

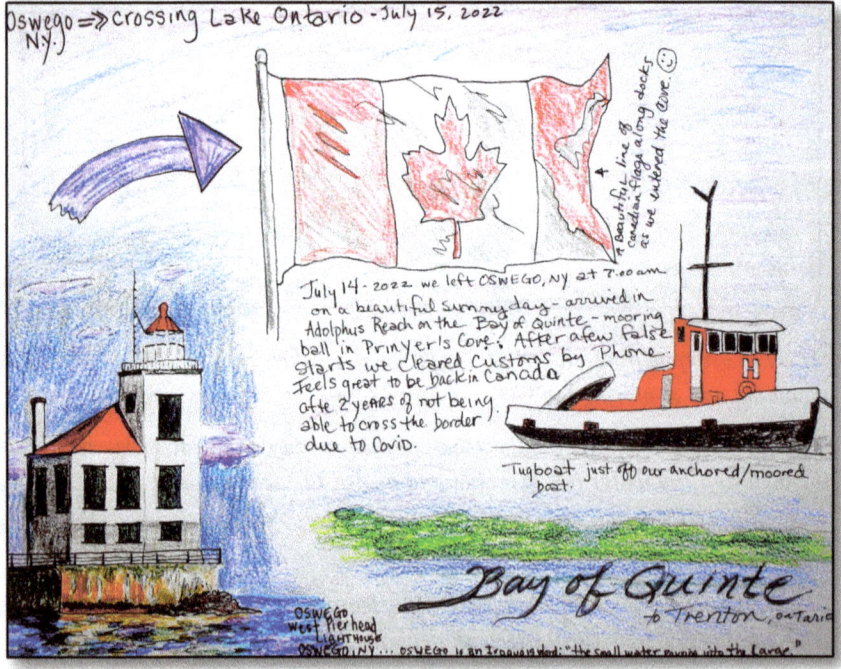

then urban fun. Blues Music. "The Last Waltz" tribute to the Band. A concert in a park just a few feet from our boat. Some of Canada's best musicians! So much talent. Also visited the Canadian Canoe Museum and a local Art Museum. I drew a lady sleeping in a canoe on the water - inspired by the historic photos I saw at the museum.

7/22 Left marina at noon, very hot, did several locks. Tied up at Lock 24. I always enjoy the free walls, besides the savings in marina costs there is always privacy and the romance of feeling like we are on a narrow boat canal trip.

7/25 Love Sick lock and wall (#30) Such a gorgeous park setting at this lock. Rocks and paths, flowers, so much natural beauty. Met a couple on a smaller trailerable boat who vacation here for several days each summer. I understand why this is a destination. All the boats gathered for social time, there were four boats in all spending the night. A fun stop. The lockmasters leave every evening

and commute back and forth to work on a boat as this is an uninhabited island with no roads. We met so many interesting loopers, boaters from Canada, the USA, and some even from Australia. Perhaps the most colorful was the crew of You N Me. I really enjoyed the colors, patterns, and bold character of this home-built Northumberland Boat.

7/27 Lock 36, the Kirkland lift lock. The second tallest lift lock in the world after the Peterborough lock. Over 100 locks so far. Illinois, Mississippi, Ohio, Tombigbee, Dismal Swamp, Erie, Oswego, and Trent Severn. Remembering how nervous I was on our first Chicago River lock. It is so brilliant to use locks as recreational parks for all people to enjoy. A three-generation family came along and set up a tent next to their small power boat and camped, had a picnic, and swam.

8/3 Big Chute Marine Railway Lock. Waited at the dock while repairs were made to the lock. Rained all day. Played Scrabble and made stir fry. Maybe tomorrow.

8/4 So smooth! It was amazing! I took a great video of this roller coaster ride. Leaving the Trent-Severn Waterway was hard as I could have stayed for years.

Georgian Bay and the North Channel

Man belongs to the earth, the earth does not belong to man.

Ojibwe saying

Georgian Bay of Lake Huron is sometimes referred to as a sixth Great Lake. Close in size to Lake Ontario it is a fabled cruising area with thousands of islands and inlets. It is a land of breath-taking vistas and heart-aching beauty. It is no wonder Indigenous people have considered this part of the world the home of the Great Spirit. There is an inside passage known as the small craft route that allows boaters to move up and down the coast while protected by the many islands from the full fury of an angry lake. The scenery is a stunning combination of rocks, trees, and clean blue water. The passages are often torturous and require the helmsperson to pay close attention. Water depths can change from 100 feet to less than 1 foot in a boat length. The bottom is unforgiving rock and there are no tides to lift the unfortunate boat off its rocky perch. A location that best exemplifies the navigational intricacies encountered here is Hangdog Channel north of Pointe au Baril in the middle of a vast shoreline called Thirty Thousand Islands.

Allow me to digress:

In the community of sailors there are those who like nothing more than to regale you with salty tales of the near-death experiences they survived on the water. This subclass of boaters defines adventure as overcoming danger, the greater the danger the greater the adventure. Over a few beers at the local watering hole a thrilling retelling of a narrow escape from certain doom embellished with detailed descriptions of storm-tossed seas, torn canvas, and jagged rocks make for an entertaining story. Of course the fact that the storyteller is sitting on a bar stool telling you this implies his survival is due to the possession of great skills and bravery, or if he is of a religious bent, a special relationship with the creator of the universe that looks after him.

Of course, there are undeniable dangers out there and only a fool or a liar will say he has never experienced fear but most of those heart-in-mouth situations can be avoided by the prudent mariner who studies his charts and pays close attention to the weather. The result of this careful approach is that most passages are pretty much drama free.

So, in the absence of real danger there are some captains that feel it necessary to inflate what little danger there is. The times I have been warned of the harrowing experience that awaited me on the loop is a long one. I was told by a perfectly sober, intelligent captain of a large motor yacht that traveling on Lake Michigan after Labor Day was a wildly reckless decision that would probably result in the loss of the boat and crew. Wow! His intention and manner were paternal, but his conclusions were inaccurate. I've been on the Great Lakes in October, and it can be perfectly pleasant if you pay attention to the weather forecasts.

Another Looper painted a terrifying picture of the Mississippi River filled with logs rushing downstream that would puncture the stoutest hull, huge tows that would not even be aware when they ran over you, and huge swirling whirlpools that would drag you to the bottom and not release you for days! It turned out to be a fun and memorable part of our journey.

Another location on the Loop whose horrific reputation are all out of proportion to the rather sedate reality and minor challenge they present yet results in much hysterical pearl clutching is the "Rock Pile." The "Rock Pile" is about a mile long stretch of the Atlantic ICW near Myrtle Beach, South Carolina. The Army Corp of Engineers had to blast its way through a section of solid rock in order to complete the waterway. The result is a narrower than usual channel whose edges are jagged rock instead of the usual soft mud. At low tide the bordering rocks are clearly visible. At high tide they lurk beneath the surface. The sailing line is clearly marked with navigational aids, and if the helmsperson stays awake and uses standard precautions there is absolutely no problem. Boats that do come to grief are usually piloted by yahoos attempting ill-advised passes of slower vessels or distracted captains wandering out of the channel. In spite of the benign nature of this passage I have heard people talk of their experience as though they had rounded Cape Horn!

Which brings us to Hang Dog Channel in Canada's Georgian Bay. This section of the well-charted "small craft route" is undeniably tight and twisty and requires careful piloting. It is important to know where you are at all times and pick out the navigational markers that lead you safely through a constellation of rocks. However, its reputation among some boaters is of a passage so treacherous that certain destruction awaits any vessel that attempts it. As a result of this misinformation, most loopers avoid it altogether and take a detour around it. By doing so they miss the pleasure of accomplishing a moderate navigational challenge and fail to see some of the most spectacular scenery on the whole loop. Jill and I found it confusing at times, on several occasions, had to consult

Sketch of Alvin James at anchor by Kara Dodge.

with each other about our planned route, but the reward was a trip through a landscape of heart-aching beauty.

My advice to those who cruise in unfamiliar water is pay attention to the stories told on the docks and bars. Much useful information can be gleaned by these chance encounters. However, keep in mind that sailors, like fishermen, tend to exaggerate. Trust your boat, trust your crew, trust your charts, and above all trust your own ability and instincts.

We spent a week alternating between marinas and pristine wilderness anchorages before arriving at the sublime Bustard Islands where we met up with old friends on their annual sailing sabbatical. For three days we swam, fished, and prepared meals together before we had to move on. We vowed to meet in a week or so farther east in the North Channel. We left for the town of Killarney, Ontario, on a beautiful sunny day when the big bay was in a benevolent mood. About eight miles off the entrance to Killarney the engine started making a god-awful racket. It sounded like it was self-destructing. We stopped and I opened the floorboards to inspect the engine compartment. There was nothing readily apparent until I crawled into the engine room on my hands and knees and squeezed myself into a position in front of the engine. The problem became obvious. The alternator arm had snapped, and the alternator destroyed itself banging against the other drive pulleys. The belts had been thrown off and there was no way I could tension the belts enough to run the water pump. We were essentially dead in the water and required a tow. We contacted Killarney but they had no towboats. I considered hip tying the dinghy to the *Alvin James* and slowly (very slowly!) motoring us into Killarney, but there were no repair facilities there either. Our radio calls were being monitored by the Canadian Coast Guard and they hailed us to get our position and current status. We told them we had lost power and were looking for a tow but were in no immediate danger. They told us they would stay in touch and would like regular updates on our situation. We were finally able to get a towboat willing to come from Little Current, more than 40 miles away. It would take about three hours to arrive, so we settled into a long wait.

There was very little wind but what there was pushed us east. The water was too deep to anchor but we decided that as soon as we drifted into a shallow area we would drop the hook. A boat that had overheard our conversation with the Coast Guard approached our position and offered help. We thanked them for their concern but said we had arranged for a tow and we were in no danger. Every half hour the Coast Guard called and asked us for an update on our position and our situation. Of course, all this radio communication was on standard VHF frequencies, so it was overheard by anyone within range of a VHF signal. The towboat arrived and passed us a line and we began a five-hour tow to Little Current. For weeks afterwards, strangers on the dock would recognize our boat name and ask about our breakdown on Georgian Bay.

The following day technicians from the marina removed the alternator, the alternator arm, and the bracket. The alternator could be rebuilt by a local shop. A new arm could be fabricated in-house. The bracket, which had also broken, was a casting and an Internet search began for a replacement. Finding a casting for a 35-year-old engine was no easy task but the crew got on it. The best-case scenario was a four-day fix, so we decided to just enjoy our stay.

Roy Eaton is famous among North Channel boaters as the voice of the Little Current Cruisers' Net. During the boating season, the Cruisers' Net broadcasts every day at 9:00 a.m. on VHF Channel 71. Roy reads the local and national news, tells stories of local interest, and finishes with a call-in from where boaters can give their positions and destinations. It is useful for keeping track of friends and is the glue that holds the boating community together. Every Friday evening in Little Current there is a Cruisers' Net meet-and-greet hosted by the Anchor Inn Hotel. Roy approached us at the meet-and-greet and said he had heard we had a major malfunction out on Georgian Bay. (Of course he had!) Knowing we were stuck in town waiting for repairs he offered us the use of his truck for the next three days so we could explore the island. We gratefully accepted his generous offer and took full advantage of the mobility.

Well dear reader, I won't bore you with the gruesome details, but the four-day estimate for repairs stretched to two weeks. Parts didn't arrive and those that did were the wrong ones. Finally in desperation we found a local machine shop that felt they could repair the damaged bracket and did. We said goodbye to Little Current and left the harbor only to stop less than a mile away with an over-heating alarm shrieking in our ears. Assuming the technicians had screwed something up, I called the Marina and demanded to be towed back in to have the problem addressed. The problem, to my great relief and my great embarrassment, was an almost complete lack of coolant! I was religious about checking oil and coolant levels before starting the engine. How could this have happened? Well, I was checking the coolant at the overflow tank but never at the filler cap that was in an almost inaccessible location in the engine room. There was an obstruction in the line from the overflow tank back to the fill tank that gave the illusion I had plenty of coolant but in fact told me nothing of value. I learned a valuable lesson. We thanked the marina people for the quick response and left the harbor again, poorer but wiser.

Later that day, we stopped in the town of Gore Bay. This was always one of our favorite stops in the North Channel and we had made many friends in the community. In fact, we had bought our boat in Gore Bay from Norm and Diane, the couple that run the boatyard. Norm is reputed to be the best mechanic in the area and the *Alvin James* was his boat before he sold it to us. I knew Norm knew my boat better than anyone and I asked him if he might spend a bit of time with me giving the mechanicals a once-over. He has a full schedule, but he made time and gave me some valuable advice. On our last night in town, we treated Norm, Diane, and several other friends to dinner at our favorite waterfront restaurant and watering hole, owned by another friend. We were on our way home now and this would be our last stop on Canadian soil until next year.

Excerpts from Jill's Sketch Journal:

8/5 On to San Souci (Georgian Bay) We saw a sign for Henry's through our binoculars and pulled up to the dock. This is a real landmark in the area - known for fish dinners. We were the only boat and then within an hour it was packed. Took a couple of swims off the sea plane landing – it was hot! Tourists pay for a seaplane ride from the mainland just for lunch at Henry's. We saw a collection of bent propellers. James called them the "Georgian Bay Flower Bed."

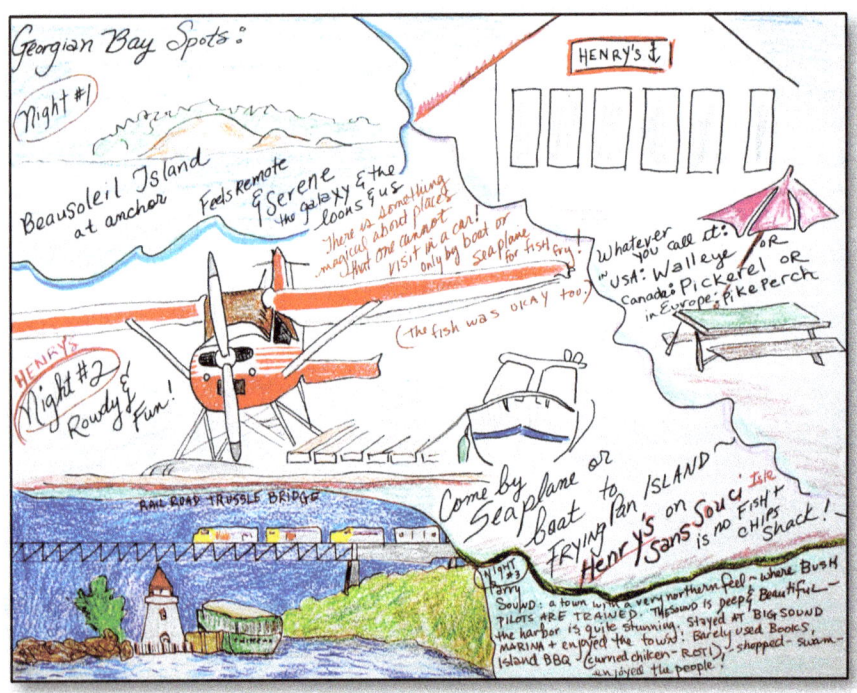

8/8 Hang Dog Channel. Bigger boats are warned not to attempt this passage. It is intense and challenging but our hard-earned skills and teamwork got us through. Out on Georgian Bay, had my only bout of sea sickness on the loop, as we bashed our way to the Bustard Islands. I had sea sickness a whole lot as a child and in our early years of sailboat cruising but happily this is now a rarity.

8/10 Very excited to be back in the Bustards and to see our dear friends Kara and Steve on Mas Encantada. Moon watching, loon watching, painting with Kara, cooking and feeding each other. Catching and eating fresh bass, Scrabble games, such a beautiful place to enjoy with our friends. We saw a few Looper companies too, including the crews of Pivot and Wildlife.

8/13 Doing a cruise with our friends on Mas Encantada, snaking through islands and rocks to a beautiful anchorage on the French River. We dropped anchor behind Obstacle Island. I painted the rocks in one of the most beautiful places on earth. Tidying the back deck before Steve and Kara come over when a gust of wind picked up one of my watercolor paintings which was drying on a cushion. It blew overboard and floated on top of the water. I rescued it with a boat hook and set it on a dry towel in the sun. No harm done — might have even improved the image.

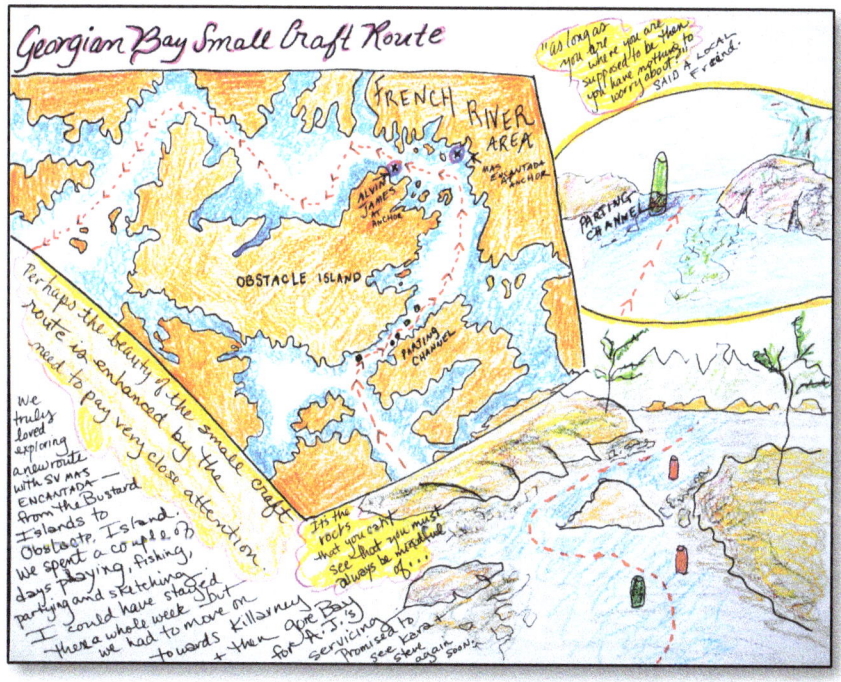

8/15 Said "See ya" to Kara and Steve and headed towards Killarney. A sudden Racket – Shut off engine – OH NO! Luckily it was a mild weather day so we floated and I made lunch while we slowly drifted towards an island. We planned to put an anchor down when shallower waters allowed. We reflected how lucky we were that this didn't happen on the small craft route on a bad weather day.

8/16–8/31 At slip in Boyles Marina, Little Current, Ontario. This is a port that feels almost like home. For many years we have docked, waited out weather, filled up our provision lockers, and attended cruiser net broadcasts and potlucks. The idea of spending a stretch of days here, waiting for repairs, was not a bad idea at all. We saw good friends. Walked the docks. I found some colorful vin-

tage geological charts at Turners department store and did some collage work with them. Hiked the Cup and Saucer Trail and did some sightseeing after Roy Eaton kindly lent us his truck. After lunch with Roy and Margaret Eaton, they took us to Margaret's First Nation home: Aundek Omni Kaning or AOK where we met Margaret's mother, Annie, a 93-year-old Ojibwe elder. She was baking bread with her niece. She explained that this was her job as a child, so being blind was not an impediment at all. I teared up meeting Annie. Although we didn't get to any of our favorite anchorages, we had a really memorable stay in Little Current as we waited for parts and repairs. The loop year offered many twists and turns that we couldn't have planned for. Because we made the best of each day, no matter what it served us, we were constantly reminded that we are not in control and it is how we react that defines our lives.

8/29 The Survivors Flag was flown in Ottawa today, honoring and remembering residential school survivors and those who died at the schools. It was good to get back to the Objibwe Cultural Center on the island with good friend and sketching partner Kara Dodge.

9/1 Left Little Current – boat fixed – Yay! Oops – not yet...A big screeching noise at Picnic Island and a tow back to Boyles Marina. The coolant tank was empty! Quick fix and we are on our way again.

9/2 It has been 1 year since we started the loop and we are at Gore Bay, Ontario, our home away from home. So, we flew our AGLA Gold Burgee and celebrated being in home waters. Pizza and cold drinks at Bouys Restaurant with Bill and Richard. We enjoyed Gore Bay. Norm took time from his packed schedule to look over the boat and declare us good to go after oil and filter changes. Though this quick visit was too short we hope to be back next summer for more of the most beautiful part of the loop – our beloved North Channel.

9/4 Trip to Vidal Bay. One last night to anchor out in Canadian waters as we await calmer waters before heading homeward.

The Great Lakes and Home

The Home Stretch
What we call the end is often the beginning.

T.S. Elliot

The wind and waves were blustery the day we left Gore Bay and headed west. Jill and I tucked into an anchorage in Vidal Bay in the lee of Vidal Island. This gave us protection from the building waves, and we spent a pleasant night. Checking the weather predictions, it seemed prudent to wait until noon before leaving. The winds were subsiding, and we wanted to give the sea state ample time to settle down. When we finally did get underway, things were a lot smoother than they had been the previous day. We crossed the Mississauga Strait separating Manitoulin Island from Cockburn Island. Crossing the False Detour Passage

on the west end of Cockburn, we entered the territorial waters of the United States. We were unsuccessful contacting U.S. Customs before anchoring in the sheltered cove of Harbor Island. Technically, you must clear in through Customs before anchoring, but our inability to communicate gave us no reasonable option. Searching the Internet, we discovered we could legally clear in at our first port of call at Mackinaw City. Our friends Cara and Steve were in Mackinaw City preparing their boat for winter storage. We planned a reunion.

The trip from Harbor Island to Mackinaw City was a downhill sleigh ride in 5-foot following seas. Boats traveling in the opposite direction were laboring and throwing up huge plumes of water over their bows, but our passage was comfortable and smooth. The entrance channel to the marina is not obvious and we motored around in the lumpy seas trying to find an opening in the huge concrete wall that protected the harbor. When we did locate the opening, it was narrow and had a sharp dogleg immediately upon entering. Combined with the rushing waves it made for a tricky few moments for the crews of boats unfamiliar with the marina.

We landed at the fuel dock and as I tended to the fueling, Jill took care of our obligations to U.S. Customs. With our chores complete we were assigned a slip and it turned out to be next to our friends on Mas Encantada. A grand reunion was had, and we celebrated with a meal in town. After vowing solemnly to get back together on dry land after our separate nautical adventures were wrapped up, we left the next day on the last leg of our journey home. Crossing under the magnificent Mackinac Bridge, we entered the waters of Lake Michigan. We continued westward over smooth seas and under a blue sky accented by brilliant white clouds. Reaching Grays Reef Passage, we turned south in the channel that marks a safe passage through this huge expanse of rocky shoal reaching halfway across the lake. Soon Beaver Island and other islands in the archipelago appeared on the horizon.

Beaver island is the largest island on Lake Michigan and also the most remote. It is almost 40 miles from the mainland and is only accessible by boat or airplane. There is a ferry that travels from Charlevoix, Michigan and back every day, and a small airfield. St. James Harbor in the northeast corner of the island is large and accommodating and is a popular waypoint for sailors going to or coming from the Straits of Mackinac. We got a slip at the marina and planned a laid-back day on the island. Jill had posted our position on Facebook, and we were immediately contacted by cousin Michael who we had last seen in Jacksonville, Florida, after an absence of 40 years. He was on Beaver Island visiting friends who had bought a home there. Another stunning coincidence! He offered to pick us up and a feast was planned at his friends' home that evening. Michael's wife is a very accomplished artist originally from South Africa who wanted to prepare a traditional South African dish for us. We had a great time and exchanged tales of adventures experienced and adventures yet to come. We also spoke of how serendipity can play a role in our lives. When we lay in our V-berth that night, Jill and I spoke about the magical and unexpected events of this year-long trip.

At dawn we left St. James Harbor and shaped a course southwest for Washington Island off the coast of Door County, Wisconsin. It was a seventy-five-mile crossing, and we were fortunate that the weather cooperated to make it a most pleasant passage. We spent the night anchored in Washington Harbor between Rock Island and Washington Island. In the morning, we traveled down Green Bay to the city of Sturgeon Bay. Since rough weather was imminent, we knew we would have to wait at least a day before venturing out on the big waters. While we were holed up, several Wisconsin friends came to visit, and we had some enjoyable reunions.

Our departure day was not ideal, but it seemed a reasonable travel day. It was lumpy and gray but the fact that we were almost home to friends and family made it almost enjoyable. We got phone calls from our sons and were informed they planned to meet us at the slip and catch our lines. When we entered the marina and approached our slip, we saw our son Miles and his sweetheart, Alexa, standing on the dock. With them were our dear friends, Randal and Selena. Our youngest son Jesse was on his way and would meet us at home. With the assistance of all, we landed the boat without incident and tied up. It was September 10, 2022, one year and ten days since we left this very spot to start our adventure. Tears of happiness were shed. It was good to be home.

Voyage Log #21
Friends and Shipmates,

Yesterday, on September 10th, we cruised under gray skies and over lumpy seas. Jill and I cruised the last leg of our journey from Sturgeon Bay to Manitowoc. By sheer luck, we were assigned the same slip we left from one year and eight days ago. We were greeted by our sons and the women they share their lives with and by dear friends Selena and Randal who keep a boat in the adjacent slip. It was so good to be home!

We slept in a king size bed and though it was comfortable, I was unaccustomed to the spaciousness. Sleeping for a year in the intimate confines of a boat's V-berth, I had grown accustomed to the physical contact unavoidable in that small space. I awoke in the middle of the night and realized that it was unnecessary to check the state of the batteries and the evolving weather forecasts and how that might affect our next day's travel plans. Not having any pressing navigational tasks, there was no reason to be awake, but it took several restless hours to achieve sleep. I'm not sure how long it will take to transition from a life of almost constant motion to one that is centered in one location. I long to see friends but feel I need another day or two to decompress.

Thanks for being virtual shipmates for the last year. See you soon.

Excerpts From Jill's Sketch Journal:

9/5 Anchor in Harbor Island, Michigan. Back in the USA.

9/6 Mackinaw City, Michigan. Straits State Harbor Marina with Kara and Steve of Mas Encantada, for laughs and a dinner on the town after frustration trying to connect with US Customs to officially check back into the country. After a nights rest we go to Beaver Island where we would join Trish and Tim at their island home and by chance run into Michael and Estella! Wow, how did this happen again?

9/9 Home! "We are made to persist. That is how we find out who we are." Tobias Wolf. A year away on an almost constantly moving boat is not like taking a conventional vacation, and so there is an adjustment to returning home. Besides not remembering what light switches turned on what lights, there were lots of things to get used to again. First of all, life is way easier. A car to shop or take a joy ride, my own washer and dryer, comfortable big bed, reclining chair, and Netflix. New routines – how can I maintain the creative time discipline? Do I really need to be calendar tied and event driven again?

So, there are things I learned from our year looping that I want to keep and even make stronger and more integrated into my land life:

1. Want to do less and have more time for just being spontaneously creative. And time for the most important people in my life.

2. I learned that the best way to build good habits is to do almost nothing each day. By this I mean small starts at things that will organically become more important to me. Just as my sketching time grew and became a regular good habit, I would go on to make body care/movement good healthy daily habits. But this means making time for these pursuits, and that means that some things have to give to make that happen. Prioritizing.

Also – it just reinforced that I married the right person, and that I am so glad we have persevered.

Epilogue

For several months after our return home we became minor D-list celebrities. Our fifteen minutes of fame included a front page story in our local newspaper that was later reprinted in the Milwaukee Journal and USA Today, three radio interviews, a spot on a Chicago television news program and a guest appearance on a popular podcast. The Wisconsin Maritime Museum hosted us as part of an evening lecture series on nautical themes. Fame, however, is a fleeting thing and it wasn't long before Jill and I were enmeshed in the familiar routine of our previous life.

A big part of the familiar routine involves our children. Those who do not have children often think that parenthood is a finite commitment. Once the kids graduate, marry, or somehow leave home, the job is finished, and mom and dad can retire to a carefree life of irresponsible leisure. Of course, the reality is once you conceive a child you are a parent until the day you die. Our two adult sons are strong intelligent men and their presence in our life is an undeniable joy. As resourceful and resilient as they are Jill and I can't help to be concerned as they navigate the post-Covid world and the mess our generation has left them. But man, I love having them around when my 20th-century brain can't quite wrap itself around setting up a new laptop or programing the TV or resetting the passwords I've managed to misplace.

Besides reconnecting with old friends, we stayed in touch with several friends we had met on the loop. Kara and Steve are old sailing buddies who shared several anchorages with us on the loop. They left their boat in the hands of a broker in Mackinac City. They stopped and visited for a few days on the drive home to Wyoming. Later Melanie and Justin (and Peggy) left their beautiful boat, *Sabot*, in Maine and took a major detour on the way to Austin, Texas to visit us. It is a tired cliché that the best thing about the Loop is the people you meet. That is undeniably true but of course it's the best thing about life itself; what a grim reality life would be without the friends we are blessed with.

So how has this year afloat changed us? There is the undeniable satisfaction that Jill and I worked as a team in the planning and execution of this epic trip. It wasn't a surprise, I mean we have been married over forty years, raised two children and managed households and careers, but the fact that we operated smoothly and efficiently in ever changing environments and faced numerous mechanical and weather related stressors with a certain aplomb re-inforces the feeling that I made the right choice when I married this woman.

What's next? No concrete plans. We hope we stay healthy enough to have adventures on the boat for years to come. So far, so good, but as Leonard Cohen once mused, I'm not in old age yet but I'm definitely in the foothills of old age. When that day inevitably comes when we sell the boat I hope Jill and I feel that we left it all on the field and there is no adventure we dreamed of that was left undone.

Acknowledgments

We are grateful to the following people for their help:

John Shea, his enthusiasm and suggestions were great motivators and more important to this project than he may realize.

Mark Mahowald whose technical mastery and generosity in helping prepare our boat for the voyage contributed greatly to its success.

Suzanne Weis for her skills as an editor and her tireless research to assure the factual accuracy this book.

Susan Murtaugh reviewed our writing and artwork and her encouragement was most important.

Don Krumpos, a talented artist who collaborated on the design of the cover.

Seaworthy Publications, Inc., our publishers, who believed in our book and were always accommodating and easy to work with.

All our friends near and far that encouraged us while on the loop and in the creation of our book.

About the Authors

Photo credit: Karen Valencia

James

Ever since I was a little boy I wanted a boat and to have adventures on the water. Even though my family had no nautical history and very little money to invest in anything as frivolous as a boat, the dream persisted. In adulthood I read everything I could about small boat voyaging. I read many 'how-to' manuals explaining the physics of sailing. I became fluent in the arcane technical language of sailors. Yet my life remained land bound and I began to doubt if I ever would sail over that mysterious horizon. We lived in the Florida Keys for eight years. One year I bought a 12-foot aluminum fishing boat with a 5 HP outboard for two hundred dollars. It was a boat that was made for small inland lakes and was absolutely unsuitable for the open water of the Keys. After scaring myself and putting my young family in jeopardy I traded the boat to a local fisherman for some lobster tails.

In the early nineties after being sideswiped by Hurricane Andrew, we moved north to Milwaukee and our financial situation improved. In 1998, I bought a small sailboat offered by a business acquaintance. Jill and I took sailing courses at the Milwaukee Community Sailing Center and our sailing life began. Retirement allowed us to expand our sailing horizons; sailing with friends in the Caribbean and spending months at a time sailing the Great Lakes. I am by nature a rather introverted, cerebral guy and while not a man of faith, my connection to the natural world is as close to a religious experience as I will ever have. For me traveling on the water is the most real interaction I can have with nature including its peacefulness, sublime beauty, and sometimes its terror.

Jill

My family's summers were spent operating a remote fly-in Canadian fish camp, where we made our own fun by the water. Having no electricity or media, we rose with the sun and took our cues from the earth. Befriending toads, climbing rocks, swimming, and creative play gave me the background experiences that make me who I am today.

Creativity and art have always been central to my life. My grandmother Margaret was a watercolorist and puppeteer who shared her talents with me. I would go on to study art in college but would lose the pleasures of being a simple maker when life demanded other things from me. Motherhood was important and fulfilling, but being a full-time worker and parent left little time for art.

The question of what to do with my life after our sons matured and work life ended was an interesting one. My first few years of retirement were focused on completing tasks in several community volunteer positions.

When we began considering doing the Great Loop I realized that letting go of all the distractions of life on land could mirror my childhood years at camp and I could make time for daily creativity. I see the world with different eyes when I am making art regularly. I would go on to use the simple tools in my art drawer and my needles and embroidery floss to reflect on the interesting world I saw from the windows of *MV Alvin James* and the results would often surprise me.

www.ingramcontent.com/pod-product-compliance
Lightning Source LLC
Chambersburg PA
CBHW072157160426
43197CB00012B/2418